BEST OF

Sydney

Charles Rawlings-Way

Best of Sydney
3rd edition – September 2004
First published – November 1999

Published by Lonely Planet Publications Pty Ltd
ABN 36 005 607 983

Australia Head Office, Locked Bag 1, Footscray, Vic 3011
☎ 03 8379 8000 fax 03 8379 8111
📧 talk2us@lonelyplanet.com.au
USA 150 Linden St, Oakland, CA 94607
☎ 510 893 8555 toll free 800 275 8555
fax 510 893 8572 📧 info@lonelyplanet.com
UK 72–82 Rosebery Avenue, London EC1R 4RW
☎ 020 7841 9000 fax 020 7841 9001
📧 go@lonelyplanet.co.uk
France 1 rue du Dahomey, 75011 Paris
☎ 01 55 25 33 00 fax 01 55 25 33 01
📧 bip@lonelyplanet.fr 📧 www.lonelyplanet.fr

This title was commissioned in Lonely Planet's Melbourne
office and produced by: **Commissioning Editor** Errol Hunt
Coordinating Editors Louise McGregor, Nancy Ianni
Coordinating Cartographer Simon Tillema **Layout
Designer** Sonya Brooke **Editor** Jackey Coyle **Cartographers**
Daniel Fennessy, Anthony Phelan, Hunor Csutoros **Managing
Cartographer** Corinne Waddell **Cover Designers** Gerilyn
Attebery, Wendy Wright **Project Manager** Kieran Grogan
Series Designer Gerilyn Attebery **Mapping Development**
Paul Piaia **Regional Publishing Manager** Kate Cody

Photographs by Lonely Planet Images (LPI) and Greg Elms
except for the following as listed: pages 9, 10, 11, 12,13,
17, 18, 22, 32, 33, 37, 38, 40, 41, 46, 48, 51, 52, 56, 69, 71,
83, 84, 86, 93, 95, 107 Glenn Beanland/LPI, pages 8, 10, 11,
14, 16, 17, 19, 20, 23, 25, 29, 35, 38, 53, 54, 60, 61, 64, 66,
85, 88, 94, 105, 109 Simon Bracken/LPI, pages 5, 7, 44, 103
Ross Barnett/LPI, page 43 Manfred Gottschalk/LPI, page 94
John Banagan/LPI, page 101 Michael Laanela/LPI, page 107
Gillianne Tedder/LPI, page 108 Richard I'Anson/LPI. **Cover
photograph** Sydney Opera House viewed from Dawes Point
Park, Glenn Beanland/LPI. All images are copyright of the
photographers unless otherwise indicated. Many of the
images in this guide are available for licensing from Lonely
Planet Images: 📧 www.lonelyplanetimages.com.

ISBN 1 74059 535 1

Printed through Colorcraft Ltd, Hong Kong.
Printed in China

Acknowledgements Sydney Train Network map © City
Rail 2004.

HOW TO USE THIS BOOK

Colour-Coding & Maps

Each chapter has a colour code along the
banner at the top of the page which is also
used for text and symbols on maps (eg all
venues reviewed in the Highlights chapter
are orange on the maps). The fold-out
maps inside the front and back covers are
numbered from 1 to 6. All sights and venues
in the text have map references; eg (3, B2)
means Map 3, grid reference B2. See p128
for map symbols.

Prices

Multiple prices listed with reviews (eg
$10/5/25) usually indicate adult/concession/
family admission to a venue. Concession prices
can include senior, student, member or coupon
discounts. Meal cost and room rate categories
are listed at the start of the Eating and Sleeping
chapters, respectively.

Text Symbols

☎	telephone
✉	address
🖳	email/website address
$	admission
☉	opening hours
ⓘ	information
🚃	train
Ⓜ	monorail
🚌	bus
⛴	ferry
🚈	MLR
Ⓟ	parking available
♿	wheelchair access
🍴	on-site/nearby eatery
🧒	child-friendly venue
Ⓥ	good vegetarian selection

Contents

From the Publisher

AUTHOR

Charles Rawlings-Way

Born in Devonshire and transported to Tasmania when he was three, Charles admired Sydney from afar for many years before mustering the nerve to ask her for a date. Her cool bars and warm beaches proved predictably seductive, and the harbour city has held an inescapable fascination for him ever since.

A lapsed architect, underrated rock guitarist, optimistic surfer and confirmed hedonist, Charles has toiled behind the scenes on Lonely Planet's *Best Of* series since its inception in 1999. He regularly flees the calmer cultures of Melbourne for a walk on Sydney's wild side, and to visit his mum.

Thanks to the following folks for their input, generosity, friendship and distraction during the creation of this book: Mona & Olivia Rawlings-Way, Warren & Nathan Jones, Lyn Jacobs, Errol Hunt, Sally O'Brien, Dani Valent, Michelle Bennett and leisure consultants Scott, Gerard, Louisa, David, Lauren and Christian.

Above all, thank you Meg for our truly inescapable fascination.

The 1st and 2nd editions of this book were written by Nikki Hall and Dani Valent.

PHOTOGRAPHER

Greg Elms

Greg's interest in photography began during a stint of winery work in the Barossa Valley, where regular wine consumption forced him to lie on his back and gaze skyward at the spectacular cloudscapes that formed above the Valley. Knowing his memory of the view would be somewhat wine-soaked, he grabbed a camera.

On completing a BA in Photography at RMIT, Greg then assisted a photographer for two years before taking off on a travel odyssey around Australia, Southeast Asia, India, East Africa, Egypt, Israel and Europe. He now freelances for magazines, graphic designers, advertising agencies, and, of course, book publishers such as Lonely Planet.

Greg was commissioned to take photos for LP's *World Food Mexico, Turkey, France, India* and *China*. He has also contributed to numerous Lonely Planet guidebooks over the past 12 years. *Best of Sydney* is his first commission for this series.

SEND US YOUR FEEDBACK

We love to hear from travellers — your comments keep us on our toes and help make our books better. Our well-travelled team reads every word on what you loved or loathed about this book. Although we cannot reply individually to postal submissions, we always guarantee that your feedback goes straight to the appropriate authors, in time for the next edition — and the most useful submissions are rewarded with a free book. To send us your updates — and find out about LP events, newsletters and travel news — visit our award-winning website: 💻 **www.lonelyplanet.com.**

Note: We may edit, reproduce and incorporate your comments in Lonely Planet products such as guidebooks, websites and digital products, so let us know if you don't want your comments published. For a copy of our privacy policy visit 💻 www.lonelyplanet.com/privacy.

Introducing Sydney

At the heart of Sydney – Australia's oldest, largest and most diverse city – is the outrageously good-looking Sydney Harbour. Like a psychedelic supermodel, the city curves and sways through this glamorous maze of lazy bays, sandstone headlands, quirky islands and legendary surf beaches.

No less culturally complex than it is on the map, Sydney is the landing point for most of Australia's immigrants. It's a multicultural, hyperactive and seductive city where you can lose yourself in the arts, restaurants, markets and dance clubs just as easily as on the streets.

Australians perceive Sydney-siders as more *carpe diem* than museum, with their minds firmly fixed on sunglasses, salons and their next soy latte. They're pretty people, but they're also motivated and confident. Outside is where it's at – the beaches swarm, street cafés buzz, national parks provide quiet solace and the harbour blooms with sails.

Coursing between the crazed geography and the blonde dye in Bondi is an infectious gutsy energy. Big-city cynicism, poverty and suburban sprawl are a reality, but raw economic enthusiasm prevails. It's no small irony that Sydney – once a cesspit dumping ground for British and Irish convicts – has evolved into a sparkling, progressive metropolis with optimism, tolerance and staggering natural beauty at the helm. Australia's capital in every sense but name, Sydney is the definitive ugly duckling turned majestic swan.

Curvaceous and sexy; layers of Sydney glamour

Neighbourhoods

Central Sydney grips Port Jackson (Sydney Harbour) in a passionate embrace, while Greater Sydney shambles over 1800 sq km from Botany Bay to the south, the Blue Mountains to the west and Pittwater to the north. The

Sipping lattes in Surry Hills, Sydney style

harbour runs east-west dividing the city in two – the Sydney Harbour Bridge and Harbour Tunnel connect the south and north shores. The city centre and most of the action are south of the harbour.

The Rocks and **Circular Quay** are tourist meccas with superb restaurants. Sydney's **CBD** burgeons with bistros, shops and cool bars that pump during the week, but the city centre is largely abandoned to the skateboarders on weekends. West of the city centre is **Chinatown** where dragons, fireworks and cultural immersion temper the shameless spruikers on Dixon St. Further west is **Darling Harbour** – an architecturally psychotic tourist haven – where boardwalks, museums, restaurants, bars, freeway

flyovers, hotel monoliths and Star City Casino distract the masses.

West of Darling Harbour are the rejuvenated once-were-warehouse suburbs **Ultimo** and **Pyrmont**. Cafés and bookshops tangle with dreadlocked bohemia in **Glebe**, while picture-perfect **Balmain** has frangipanifilled laneways, beery pubs and rambling rows of million-dollar cottages. Grungy **Newtown** is King of the Inner West – tattoos, tofu, students and sexual subculture rule on King St. Italian restaurant-goers in Italian cars cruise the Italian Forum (aka Armani Arena) in Norton St **Leichhardt**.

Strutting your stuff down George St, The Rocks

Rock 'n' roll ain't noise pollution in **Annandale**, but the jumbos are a headache.

East of the city are **East Sydney** and **Darlinghurst** – cafés bulge with cinematographers, thespians and gym-junkies buffing up for Mardi Gras.

Formerly a slum full of drunks, sailors and drunk sailors, **Woolloomooloo** offers brilliant restaurants and relaxed pubs. **Surry Hills** brims with great places to eat and drink and bears absolutely no resemblance to Surry. **Kings Cross** stews in its sleazy, strangely hypnotic brand of sex, drugs and rock 'n' roll, while **Potts Point** (just a block away) is all classy restaurants, private-school girls and security entrances. **Paddington** has gorgeous terrace houses, avantgarde galleries and everything is pretty in pink on Oxford St.

The Eastern Suburbs are affluent and monocultural. In **Woollahra** summer chestnuts hang heavy on the bough and kids say 'Hey, nice BMW!' Bay St in **Double Bay** is a shimmering vision of Range Rovers and skinny models. **Vaucluse** shelters surgeons in Volvos from too much real world; **Watsons Bay** surfs waves of mortgage madness on the Pacific rim. Head to **Bondi Junction** for all your yoga, whale music and wheatgerm requirements.

To the southeast of these is the quintessential ocean suburb **Bondi** (surfboards, sushi, Internet, beer – take your pick). Further south are sexy **Tamarama**, family **Bronte** and backpacker **Coogee**.

North of the Harbour Bridge is the North Shore business district – a city unto itself – beyond which middle-class suburbia sprawls reservedly. The prime minister's and

> ## Off the Beaten Track
> All that buzz and business stressing you out? Vamoose to:
> - **Rushcutters Bay Park** (6, D3) Chill out on waterfront lawns where the pontoons bump and sway.
> - **Balmoral** (p32) Some tasty restaurants and an ace place for a swim.
> - **Millers Point** (5, B3) Just west of the Rocks frenzy are calm terraces, unpretentious pubs and the Sydney Observatory.
> - **Jubilee Park** (2, B4) At the Glebe Point Rd end, snooze in the sun, throw a frisbee or get stuck into your airport novel under a gargantuan Moreton Bay fig.

Calm before the Sydney storm, Millers Point

governor general's Sydney mansions are in posh, influential **Kirribilli**. Advertising execs in **McMahons Point** lunch on café-lined Blues Point Rd, named after 1830s Jamaican ferryman Billy Blue. West of the Harbour Bridge is **Milsons Point**, famous for the iconic and sporadically operational Luna Park. The jewel of the North Shore is **Manly** – the surf's as good as the kebabs. The magnificent **Northern Beaches** stretch north from here – 30km of sandy suburbs, rocky headlands and gnarly surf beaches.

Itineraries

If you've only got a day or three to make Sydney's acquaintance, try the following itineraries. Most of Sydney's many signature attractions make the grade here, along with some rewarding local hangouts. They're all in the city or inner suburbs and are easily accessible on foot or by public transport – for which a three, five or seven-day SydneyPass (p111) is a stellar idea.

Worst of Sydney

- Wheezy air, aircraft cacophony and harbour junk.
- Attitude – big fish in a small pond; watch them ooze 'tude.
- Tacky Australiana shops and colonial cash-in.
- Sunburn – the southern sun kicks like a mule.
- Party, party, party... Don't you people read books?
- Gnarly rips at the beach – swim between the flags!
- Cockroaches – things that go crunch in the night.

Rip it up in the surf, Manly

Day One

Ramble down through The Rocks to Sydney Cove then out past the Sydney Opera House to the Royal Botanic Gardens. Grab a cab to Bondi Beach and dunk yourself in the Pacific. Catch an evening show at the Opera House then chill on Circular Quay with some fresh seafood, divine Australian wine and harbour hubbub.

Hobnobbing at Circular Quay

Day Two

Kick-start your day/heart with a BridgeClimb (p47) over the Sydney Harbour Bridge. Vertigo? Check out the Aboriginal & Torres Strait Islander exhibition at the Art Gallery of NSW. Ship yourself out onto the harbour: take a ferry to Taronga Zoo, or to Manly for a surf. Chow down on The Wharf at Woolloomooloo then hit some slick Darlinghurst bars for a jazzy nightcap or four.

Day Three

Ogle the fashions on Paddington's Oxford St, then head to Vaucluse House and Watsons Bay for harbour scenes and fish and chips for lunch. Water taxi it back to the city and soar up Sydney Tower for jaw-dropping 360° views. Immerse yourself in a Chinatown soup then cool your boots in the boardwalk bars at Darling Harbour.

Highlights

BONDI BEACH

Bondi – where ocean and land collide; where the Pacific Ocean arrives in great foaming swells; where all people are equal, as democratic as sand. Definitively Sydney, Bondi is one of the world's great beaches.

In pre-rollerblade days, Bondi's flavour came from the Jewish, Italian and British immigrants who populated the Eastern Suburbs. Bondi has become irresistibly hip – surfers, models, skate punks, backpackers and Japanese tourists now ride a hedonistic wave through all the pubs, bars and restaurants on **Campbell Parade**. Housing prices on Bondi's strangely treeless slopes have rocketed through the stratosphere, but the beach is a priceless constant.

Bondi is the closest ocean beach to the city centre, has consistently good (though crowded) waves and

INFORMATION

(i) January's Flickerfest short film festival happens at the Bondi Pavilion; September's Festival of the Winds fills the sky with kites; November's Sculpture by the Sea is an art-fest on the clifftop trail

🚌 380, 389 or L82 from Circular Quay, 381-2 from Bondi Junction

✗ p64-5

Waiting for the perfect set

Stats on the Beach

- Bondi is 950m long and 100m wide at its southern end – the widest beach in Sydney.
- The average water temperature is 21°C.
- 3000 bedraggled swimmers are rescued from the surf annually, mostly after being caught in rips.
- Bondi has Australia's two oldest surf lifesaving clubs: Bondi Surf Bathers' Club (1906) and North Bondi (1907).
- 276 removable concrete pylons were driven into the sand for the 2000 Olympics' Beach Volleyball competition.

is great for a rough 'n' tumble swim. If the sea's angry, head for the saltwater sea baths at either end of the beach (also great for kids). More cultural centre than boat shed, the 1929 Mediterranean/Georgian-revival **Bondi Pavilion** (3, B1; ☎ 8362 3400; www.waverley.nsw .gov.au) offers change rooms, showers, outdoor cinema, exhibitions and live performances. Nearby is Sunday's **Bondi Beach Market** (p49).

Check out the **Aboriginal rock engravings** near the cliffs at the Bondi Beach Golf Club (p116) just north of the beach – the name 'Bondi' derives from an Aboriginal word for the sound of the surf.

Heading south, a majestic **clifftop trail** (p39) passes Tamarama and Bronte, continuing to Clovelly and Coogee beaches and **Waverley Cemetery** (2, E6; ☎ 9665 4932; www.waverley.nsw.gov.au/cemetery; ☼ 7am-dusk) where writer Henry Lawson and cricketer Victor Trumper are among the subterranean.

SYDNEY HARBOUR (2)

When convicted murderer Francis Morgan stood on the gallows at Pinchgut Island in 1797, about to be strung up, he wistfully gazed out across Sydney Harbour and uttered, 'Well, you have here indeed a most beautiful harbour.' Francis had a point. The harbour is the shimmering watery soul of Sydney, its beaches, coves, bays and waterside parks providing crucial relief from the ordeals of urban life. Crisscrossed by ferries and carpeted by yachts on weekends, it's both the city's playground and a major port. The harbour's perilous cliffs, sandstone headlands, craggy islands and sandy bays stretch 20km inland to the mouth of the Parramatta River.

INFORMATION

- ⓘ NPWS @ Cadman's Cottage (5, D3; ☎ 9247 5033; www.npws.nsw.gov.au; 110 George St, The Rocks; ☉ 9.30am-4.30pm Mon-Fri, 10am-4.30pm Sat & Sun); @ Nielsen Park (2, E3; ☎ 9337 5511)
- 🚆 🚌 ⛴ Circular Quay
- ♿ good access to ferries

The **Sydney Harbour National Park** (2, F2) protects the scattered pockets of bushland around the harbour and provides some magical tracks for walking. The chardonnay way to experience Sydney Harbour is to go sailing, but if you're scant on nautical know-how there are plenty of other options. Catch the ferry to Manly (p23), take a shark-proof dip in Shark Bay (2, E3), hoof it along the stupendous Manly Scenic Walkway (p41), dine with a view at Watsons Bay (p78), Balmoral (p78) or Circular Quay (p76), or take a harbour cruise.

Five islands in Sydney Harbour are also part of the national park. **Clark Island** (2, D4) off Darling Pt, **Shark Island** (2, E4) off Rose Bay and **Rodd Island** (2, A4) in Iron Cove make for serene picnic escapes. **Goat Island** (2, C3) was once a hellish convict gulag, while **Fort Denison** (2, D3), the small fortified island just off Mrs Macquaries Pt, was a sorry site of suffering used to isolate recalci-

Sydney Harbour – get into it

trant convicts (nicknamed 'Pinchgut' for its meagre rations). Paranoid fears of a Russian invasion during the mid-19th-century Crimean War led to its fortification.

The National Parks and Wildlife Service runs the **Sydney Harbour National Park Information Centre** at Cadman's Cottage (above). Book here for tours to Goat Island (p36), Fort Denison ($22/18) and other islands ($5 landing fee; suss out your own transport). Tours to the harbour's largest island, **Cockatoo Island** (2, B3), are run by the Harbour Trust (☎ 8969 2199 Tue & Wed; $25/15; ☺ Sat & Sun morning & afternoon).

Forming the gateway to Sydney Harbour are **North Head** and **South Head** (2, F2). **Watsons Bay** (2, E3) nestles on South Head's harbour side – surrounded by part of Sydney Harbour National Park, it fosters a salty cottage atmosphere. On the ocean side of South Head is **The Gap** (2, F3) – an epic clifftop lookout where sunrises, sunsets, canoodling and suicide leaps transpire with similar frequency.

North of Watsons Bay on the harbour side are two small beaches: **Lady Bay** (p33) a mainly gay, nudist beach, and **Camp Cove** (p32) a pretty photogenic swimming beach where Arthur Phillip first landed. There is a first-rate walking track from Camp Cove passing through Lady Bay, Inner South Head and The Gap, ending on windswept Outer South Head with sweeping harbour views to North and Middle Head.

Make like a salmon and chase the harbour upstream to Parramatta (p45) on a flat-bottomed **RiverCat** (☎ 9207 3170; www.sydneyferries.info; Wharf 5, Circular Quay; $7/3.50; ☺ 9am-7.20pm Mon-Fri, 8am-7pm Sat & Sun) – an ingeniously lazy way to check out the harbour's upper reaches.

DON'T MISS
- Fish and chips at **Doyles**, Watsons Bay (p78).
- A dawn or dusk kiss at **The Gap**.
- A **harbour** island tour or picnic.
- Kilometres of mansions, rugged coast and speccy views on the **Manly Scenic Walkway** (p41).

Lovers' Leap – pucker up at The Gap

Doyles at Watsons Bay – Sydney Harbour never tasted so good

SYDNEY OPERA HOUSE (5, E2)

Australia's most recognisable icon and mandatory sight squats theatrically on Bennelong Point. A celestial piece of architecture, the Opera House is gorgeous from any angle, but the view from a ferry coming into Circular Quay is hard to beat. Danish architect Jørn Utzon's 1956 competition-winning design is mused to have drawn inspiration from orange segments, sails, shells, palm fronds and Mayan temples, and has been poetically likened to a typewriter stuffed with scallop shells and the emotional congress of white turtles shagging.

The predicted four-year construction started in 1959, and after a tumultuous tirade of ego clashes, technical difficulties and delays, the Opera House was finally opened in 1973. The 67m-high roof features 27,230 tonnes of Swedish tiles (1,056,000 of them). 2300 annual performances cost over $40 million to run and keep the Concert Hall organ's 10,500 pipes humming.

There are four main auditoriums where dance, concerts, opera and theatre are staged (p90). Many events sell out quickly, but there are often short notice 'partial view' tickets available. There's also an **Exhibition Hall** and an artsy-craftsy **Sunday market** (p49) on the concourse. **Kids at the House** features kids' music, dance and drama including the Babies' Proms Orchestra and introductory ballet with Australian Ballet dancers. The bi-monthly *Opera House Diary* is available free.

INFORMATION

☎ 9250 7111,
box office 9250 7777

💻 www.sydneyopera
house.com.au

💲 free to building; performance prices vary

🕑 box office 9am-
8.30pm Mon-Sat, 2½
hours pre-show Sun

ℹ️ Front of House Tour
(☎ 9250 7250;
$20/14; 🕑 1hr
tour 8.30am-5pm);
infrequent Backstage
Tour ($30)

🚃 🚌 ⛴ Circular Quay

♿ good (☎ 9250 7250
for info)

🅿 carpark available

🍴 Guillaume at
Bennelong (p68)

The Soap Opera House

The Opera House construction hullabaloo featured uncompromising artistic vision, delays, politicking and cost blowouts. Utzon's heavenly design collided with politechnical turmoil in the '60s – Utzon quit in disgust in 1966 as the NSW government fumbled $102 million costs. The debacle continued: a possum graced the stage during opening night rehearsals and stage elevators entrapped actors.

The aftermath has been smooth, high arts complemented with cameos by Ray Charles, Billy Connolly, *Star Trek* conventions and the 1981 Mr Universe competition. Opera Australia's 1995 epic *The Eighth Wonder* dramatised Utzon's escapades – unembittered, he's agreed to act as prodigal consultant for an internal refit.

SYDNEY HARBOUR BRIDGE (5, D1)

Whether they're driving over it, climbing up it, rollerblading across it or sailing under it, Sydneysiders adore their bridge and swarm around it like ants on ice cream. Dubbed the 'old coat hanger', it's a spookily big object – moving around Sydney you'll catch sight of it in the corner of your eye and get a fright.

The bridge links the Sydney CBD with the North Sydney business district, crossing the harbour

> **INFORMATION**
> ✉ access stairs via The Rocks (Cumberland St) or North Shore (Milsons Point Train Station)
> 💲 pedestrians free; $3 for southbound vehicles
> ℹ Pylon Lookout Museum (☎ 9240 1100; www.pylonlookout.com.au; $8.50/3; ☉ 10am-5pm)
> 🚉 🚢 Circular Quay, Milsons Point
> ♿ no (stairs to footpath)

> **Coat Hanger Compendium**
> - The sandstone pylons perform no structural function; they were built to make the bridge look safe.
> - The bridge is 134m high and 502m long.
> - 1400 workers took nine years to build it.
> - 16 builders died in construction accidents.
> - A makeover takes 10 years and 30,000L of paint.
> - It weighs nearly 53,000 tonnes.
> - Six million bolts hold it together; the solid-gold bolt remains elusive.

at one of its narrowest points. The two halves of the mighty arch were built outwards from each shore, supported by cranes. In 1932 after nine years of merciless toil, the ends of the two arches were only centimetres apart, ready for ultimate union, when 100km/h winds set them swaying. The coat hanger hung tough and the arch was soon completed. The bridge cost $20 million, a bargain by modern standards, but the city took over 60 years to pay it off.

The best way to experience the bridge is on foot – don't expect much of a view crossing by car or train. Staircases lead up to the bridge from both shores and a footpath runs all the way across. If the footpath view doesn't sate you, try a knee-trembling **BridgeClimb** (p47) or scale the 200 stairs inside the southeast pylon to the **Pylon Lookout Museum** (above).

THE ROCKS (5, D3)

The Rocks – the site of Sydney's first European settlement – has evolved unrecognisably from its squalid, overcrowded origins. Residents once sloshed through open sewers and alleyways festered with disease, prostitution and drunken lawlessness. Sailors, whalers and rapscallions boozed and brawled shamelessly in countless harbour-side pubs.

INFORMATION

📖 www.therocks.com

ℹ️ Sydney Visitor Centre (5,D3; ☎ 9240 8788; www.sydneyvisitor centre.com; 106 George St; 🕒 9am-6pm); The Rocks Walking Tours (5,D3; ☎ 9247 6678; Shop 4 Kendall La)

🚆 🚌 🚢 Circular Quay

♿ difficult

🍴 p76

The Rocks remained a commercial and maritime hub until shipping services left Circular Quay in the late 1800s. A bubonic plague outbreak in 1900 continued the decline. Construction of the Harbour Bridge in the '20s brought further demolition, entire streets disappearing under the bridge's southern approach.

Redevelopment since the 1970s has turned The Rocks into a sanitised, historical tourist trap of cobbled streets, renovated colonial buildings, kitsch cafés and a gazillion tourist shops hocking stuffed koalas and Opera House key-rings.

Cadman's Cottage (5, D3; ☎ 9247 5033; www.npws.nsw.gov.au; 110 George St; free; 🕒 9.30am-4.30pm Mon-Fri, 10am-4.30pm Sat & Sun), built on a buried beach, is Sydney's oldest house (1816). Namesake John Cadman was Government Coxswain (boat and crew superintendent). Water Police detained nefarious types here in the 1840s, it was later converted into a home for retired sea captains. Further along George St is the weekend **Rocks Market** (p49).

Dating from 1844, **Susannah Place** (5, D3; ☎ 9241 1893; 58-64 Gloucester St; $7/3/17; 🕒 10am-5pm Sat & Sun, by appointment Mon-Fri) is a terrace of tiny houses with a tiny shop selling tiny historical wares. It's typical of the claustrophobic housing once standard in The Rocks.

The Rocks Market: less trash, more treasure

The **Argyle Stores** (1826–81; p50) on Argyle St once housed imported liquor; today it's shops and studios. West along Argyle St is the **Argyle Cut** (5, C3), a tunnel impressively excavated by convicts. On the far side of the Cut is Millers Point (5, B3), a relaxed district of early colonial homes. **Garrison Church** (5, C3) was Australia's first church (1848) and where Australia's first prime minister, Edmund Barton, became a learned gent. The church faces **Argyle Place** (5, C3), an English-style village green on which any Australian has the legal right to graze livestock. Nearby on Kent St the **Lord Nelson Brewery Hotel** (p81) and the **Hero of Waterloo** on Windmill St (5, C3) jostle for supreme respect as Australia's oldest pub. Longingly named after a Scottish riverbank, the high-brow gallery **Clyde Bank** (5, D2; ☎ 9241 4776; 43 Lower Fort St; $8; ☽ 10am-6pm Wed Sat) displays early colonial art and furniture in a restored mansion.

Built in the 1850s, the **Sydney Observatory** (5, C3; ☎ 9217 0485; www.sydneyobservatory.com.au; Watson Rd; free; ☽ 10am-5pm) observes the harbour atop Observatory Park. The colony's first windmill was built here (1796) but its canvas sails were pilfered and it eventually collapsed. The Observatory houses Australia's oldest working telescope (1874), a **3-D Space Theatre** ($6/4/16; ☽ 2.30 & 4.30pm Mon-Fri, 11am, noon, 2pm & 3.30pm Sat & Sun) and an interactive Australian Astronomy exhibition of Aboriginal sky stories and modern stargazing. Squint at galaxies far, far away during **Night Viewings** ($15/12/40; ☽ via booking). If you're feeling more earthly, Observatory Park is great for a terrestrial picnic.

Oldest ales: Lord Nelson Brewery Hotel

Formerly the Military Hospital and Fort St High School, The National Trust Centre on Watsons Rd houses the **SH Ervin Gallery** (p30) exhibiting invariably rewarding Australian art.

The waterfront between Dawes Point (5, D2) and Darling Harbour (5, B6) was once shipping-central. Darling Harbour has been redeveloped, and the Dawes Point wharves are rapidly emerging from prolonged decay. The **Wharf Theatre** (5, C2; ☎ 9250 1700; Pier 4, 22 Hickson Rd) houses the renowned **Sydney Theatre Company** (p89), **Bangarra Dance Theatre** (p89), **Australian Theatre for Young People** (p36) and **Sydney Dance Company** (p90). The shiny new **Sydney Theatre** (p89) is across the road.

DARLING HARBOUR (5, B6)

This rambling, purpose-built, waterfront tourist park lining Cockle Bay on the city's western edge was once an industrious dockland with factories, warehouses and shipyards. These days, the official spiel promotes more leisurely industry: 'Clubs, Pubs, Movies, Music, Hotels, Shopping, Dining, Attractions, Lifestyle'.

INFORMATION

- 🖥 www.darling harbour.com
- ℹ Darling Harbour Visitor Centre (☎ 9240 8788; www.sydney visitorcentre.com.au; ⏱ 10am-6pm)
- 🚉 Town Hall
- Ⓜ Darling Park
- 🚇 Convention
- 🚢 Darling Harbour
- ♿ good
- ✖ p66

Dotted between an architectural spoil of flyovers, fountains, sculptures and sailcloth are some great **museums** and **sights**, and the **Harbourside Shopping Centre** (5, B6). The snazzy **Cockle Bay Wharf** (5, B7) and **King Street Wharf** (5, B6) precincts contain a dangerous array of cafés, bars and restaurants for when you're all museumed-out.

DON'T MISS

- Nautical adventures at the **Australian National Maritime Museum** (p28).
- The ever-popular **Powerhouse Museum** (p27).
- Underwater wonderment at the **Sydney Aquarium** (p28).

Built according to the balanced principles of Yin and Yang, the **Chinese Garden of Friendship** (5, C8; ☎ 9281 6863; $6/3/15; ⏱ 9.30am-5.30pm) is an oasis of tranquillity. Designed by architects from Guangzhou (Sydney's sister city) for Australia's bicentenary in 1988, the garden interweaves pavilions, waterfalls, lakes and paths. Have your photo taken in Chinese opera costume or savour some tea and cake at the Chinese Teahouse by the lotus pond.

West of Darling Harbour is Pyrmont (5, A6), home to the **Good Living Grower's Market** (p56), the **Sydney Fish Market** (p57) and the playground of bigger fish, **Star City Casino** (p88).

Darling Harbour and Pyrmont are serviced by Monorail and MLR. A dinky people-mover train connects the sights ($3.50/2.50). Don't forget the harbour itself – below the soulless tourist flocks and belligerent ibises, it remains unflappably placid.

ROYAL BOTANIC GARDENS (5, E5)

The Royal Botanic Gardens (RBG) were established in 1816 as the colony's first vegetable patch. Today the RBG maintains a relaxed attitude – signs say, 'Please walk on the grass. We also invite you to smell the roses, hug the trees, talk to the birds and picnic on the lawns'.

Highlights in the RGB include the old-fashioned **rose garden**, the **South Pacific plant collection**, the prickly **arid garden**, the tropical **glass pyramid** and the sinister dangling **bat colony** (a murder of bats?). Kids love **Kids' Zone** tours and talks (p37). Go exploring, or just chill out on the grass. A trackless train does a circuit if you've outdone yourself strolling.

Functioning as a lookout long before Europeans arrived, **Mrs Macquaries Point** (2, C4) was named in 1810 when Elizabeth, Governor Macquarie's wife, ordered a stone chair chiselled into the rock from which she'd observe the harbour.

INFORMATION

☎ 9231 8111

🖥 www.rbgsyd.nsw
.gov.au

✉ Mrs Macquaries Rd

$ free

🕑 7am-8pm

ℹ RBG Visitors Centre
(☎ 9231 8125;
🕑 9.30am-5pm)

🚆 Circular Quay, Martin
Place

🚌 🚢 Circular Quay

♿ good (RBG Visitors
Centre maps show
access)

🍴 Botanic (5, F5;
☎ 9241 2419;
🕑 9.30-11am Sat &
Sun, noon-3pm daily)

Bats Out of Hell

Cast an eye to the Sydney dusk sky and you'll likely see the silent spectral swoop of a fruit bat on the wing. Actually, calling them bats is a misnomer – they're grey-headed flying foxes *(Pteropus policephalus)*, nocturnal mammals who roam up to 50km in search of food, returning to roost in vast, chattering colonies during the day. Vampire-esque 1m wingspans can make the blood run cold, but don't fret, they'd rather suck on a fig than your jugular.

Governing the gardens' north-west section is **Government House** (5, E3; ☎ 9931 5222; free; 🕑 10am-3pm Fri-Sun, grounds to 4pm), a Gothic sandstone mansion retaining its English-style grounds and uninterrupted harbour views. The impressive, fussy furnishings reflect the procession of governors' varying tastes. Look for paintings by Streeton, Roberts and Drysdale.

The Domain (5, E6) is the large grassy area linking the RBG to Hyde Park, preserved by Governor Phillip in 1788 for public recreation. The **Art Gallery of NSW** (p36) is here, and the lawns host free **summer concerts** (p90), Sunday's eccentric **Speakers' Corner** (p36), and **Carols by Candlelight** every Christmas.

CHINATOWN (5, C8)

Wedged between the CBD and Darling Harbour around **Dixon St**, Sydney's Chinatown is a tight nest of restaurants, shops, aroma-filled alleyways and signs in Chinese script. It's the perfect place to snap up a glitzy mobile phone-cum-MP3 player, the latest Hong Kong martial arts DVD, your fave Canto-Pop CD or a steaming plate of barbecued duck.

INFORMATION

- 🚉 Central
- Ⓜ Powerhouse Museum
- 🚉 Haymarket
- 🚌 George St buses
- ✕ p66

Chinatown goes berserk during **Chinese New Year** in late January/early February – the streets throng with sideshows, digitally accompanied musicians and stalls selling everything from good-luck tokens to black-sesame ice-cream burgers (seeing jaunty fire-breathing paper dragons after eating these is not a hallucinogenic effect).

Hungry? Spend a small fortune at an outstanding Chinese restaurant, succumb to spruiker suggestion

Chinese Whispers

The Chinese first came to Australia in 1840 when convict transport ceased and labouring jobs became freely available. Thousands more arrived during the 1850s gold rush, but when the notorious 1861 White Australia policy was enacted, immigration stalled.

In the 1870s Sydney's Chinese community gravitated to Dixon St, which rapidly became a commercial centre infamous for opium dens and gambling. Current Chinese immigration numbers are strong, and Chinese dialects are Sydney's second-most spoken.

at a mid-range Dixon St footpath emporium or chow down in a food court for next to nothing. Weekend yum cha is an essential experience, but be prepared to queue for a table at some of the more popular places. Thai, Vietnamese, Malaysian, Japanese and Korean eateries are also common, and if you head north to Liverpool St, there's a cluster of Spanish tapas bars.

Shopping in Chinatown is fun too – whether you're on the scent of some incense or a pseudo-Gucci bag, you'll find it here. Chinatown also encompasses **Paddy's Market** (p49), a Sydney institution that offers the usual market fare at rock-bottom prices.

The **Chinese Garden of Friendship** (p16), over the Liverpool St bridge in Darling Harbour, is too serene for words (so shut up and be still).

Solitude and serenity at the Chinese Garden of Friendship

KINGS CROSS & SURROUNDS (6, B2)

Riding above the CBD under the big **Coca-Cola sign** (as much a Sydney icon as LA's Hollywood sign), 'the Cross' is a bizarre, densely populated dichotomy of good and evil. Strip joints, tacky tourist shops and backpacker hostels bang heads with classy restaurants, designer cafés and gorgeous guesthouses as the Cross pumps 24/7. A weird cross-section of society is drawn to the lights – buskers, beggars, tourists, prostitutes, pimps, groomed metrosexuals, horny businessmen and underfed artists roam the streets on equal footing.

INFORMATION

- Kings Cross
- 323-7, 324-5, 333
- tourist information office (6, C2; ☎ 9368 0905; 21 Darlinghurst Rd)
- p70 and p73

In the early 19th century, Kings Cross was mostly grand estates. Gardens were subdivided in the 1840s and terrace houses sprung up. A wine-stained bohemian element moved in during the 1930s, including treasured poet Kenneth Slessor. The suburb's reputation as Australia's vice capital congealed during the Vietnam War, when American sailors (stationed at Woolloomooloo) flooded the Cross with a tide of bawdy debauchery.

The Cross retains a sleazy, cannibalistic aura and a vague sense

The Cross: welcome to the jungle...

of menace hangs in the air. Sometimes the razzle-dazzle has a sideshow appeal; sometimes walking up Darlinghurst Rd is a nauseating experience. Either way, not far from the neon, door thugs and sex shows, you'll find great restaurants, funky bars and gracious tree-lined streets; neighbouring Potts Point and Elizabeth Bay are affluent and classy (**Elizabeth Bay House** is a must-see; p26). Well-preserved Victorian, Edwardian and Art Deco houses and flats flank picturesque avenues like Victoria St, Macleay St, Llankelly Pl, Springfield Ave and Roslyn St – many owe their existence to antidevelopment 'Green Ban' protests in the 1970s.

Darlinghurst & Woolloomooloo

Smitten with a hooker in his love-hate ode 'Darling It Hurts', brilliant Aussie songwriter Paul Kelly sang, 'Darling it hurts to see you down in Darlinghurst tonight'. Kings Cross prostitutes rarely venture across William St into Darlinghurst these days – there are too many aspiring cinematographers and caffeinated students wanting to smell the action but not necessarily get involved.

Woolloomooloo (show me another word with eight 'o's) down **McElhone Stairs** from the Cross, is also cleaning up. **Harry's Cafe de Wheels** (p73) and the sailors are still there, but **The Wharf** redevelopment heralds 'money'. Things are begrudgingly less pugilistic than in the past.

SYDNEY TOWER   (5, D6)

A typical reaction from a Sydney first-timer: 'Hey, check out that gigantic tower thing in the city!' It's true, Sydney Tower is about as high as Sydneysiders get without wings or drugs, and the 360° views from the **Observation Deck** are unbeatably tall (just over 250m). Sydney is geographically befuddling – a birds-eye view is the perfect way to get a handle on the land. On a clear day you'll see west to the Blue Mountains, south to Botany Bay, east across the length of the harbour to the silvery Pacific and down onto Sydney's streets and roofs. Watch rain squalls shift across the suburbs on a stormy day.

Take the 40-second ear-popping lift ride right up the 76 floors to the top. Peer through super-strength binoculars or join free guided tours to help you spy your cousin's orange roof tiles in Glebe (anti-glare windows make for good photos). The tower has two telecommunication levels, three plant levels and two **revolving restaurants**.

INFORMATION

- ☎ 9223 0933
- 🖳 www.sydneyskytour.com.au
- ✉ 100 Market St
- 💲 22/15.85/39-67
- 🕒 9am-10.30pm
- ℹ free guided tours
- 🚆 St James
- Ⓜ City Centre
- ♿ good
- 🅿 Piccadilly car park (☎ 9264 1467; 137 Castlereagh St; discount for tower restaurant diners)
- 🍴 Skylounge Coffee Shop & International Revolving Restaurant (☎ 8223 3800; www.sydney-tower-restaurant.com)

Sydney on high

Towering Statistics

- Construction began in 1970, the tower opening in August 1981.
- The shaft is designed to withstand earthquakes and once-every-500-years freak winds.
- There's a 162,000L water tank on top which acts as a stabiliser on windy days.
- If the strands of the 56 support cables were laid end-to-end they'd reach from Sydney to New Zealand.
- The turret can hold 960 people, the three lifts shuttling 2000 gob-smacked observers per hour.
- Fancy a workout? 1504 stairs await you…

You can dine while slowly rotating above the twinkling harbour city – a truly mesmerising experience.

To scale the tower, enter the Centrepoint arcade on Pitt St Mall and follow the signs up the escalators to the ticket booths and lifts. Tickets include admission to **Skytour**, a revolving 3-D virtual-rollercoaster audio/visual extravaganza – you might love it, or you might cringe with unutterable embarrassment.

ART GALLERY OF NSW (5, F6)

Playing a prominent and gregarious role in Sydney society is the ultra-reputable Art Gallery of NSW. Established in 1874 as part of the NSW Academy of Art, five trustees were appointed to administer a £500 grant from the NSW government towards 'the formation of a gallery of art'. The trustees took the ball and ran with it, procuring a steady steam of impressive paintings, initially just from Sydney and London artists. The gallery's vision expanded, and the first steps towards establishing an indigenous art collection were made in the 1950s and early '60s.

Architecturally challenging extensions to the gallery's classical sandstone buildings in the 1970s

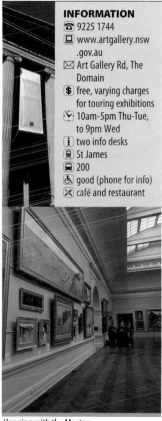

Hanging with the Masters

INFORMATION
- ☎ 9225 1744
- 🖳 www.artgallery.nsw.gov.au
- ✉ Art Gallery Rd, The Domain
- 💲 free, varying charges for touring exhibitions
- ◔ 10am-5pm Thu-Tue, to 9pm Wed
- ⓘ two info desks
- 🚇 St James
- 🚌 200
- ♿ good (phone for info)
- 🍴 café and restaurant

DON'T MISS
- Aboriginal and Torres Strait Islander art and performance at the **Yiribana Gallery**.
- Sunday tours of the Asian Gallery with **Zhenmu Shou**, a fierce but friendly guide from the grave.
- Classic Australian paintings by Brett Whiteley, Arthur Streeton, Sidney Nolan and Lloyd Rees.
- Sunday afternoon's **Speakers Corner** (p36) on the lawns in front of the gallery.

and '90s swelled the gallery's ambition. Today, blockbuster international touring exhibitions arrive regularly (Man Ray, Caravaggio etc) and the gallery lays claim to the most broadly representative collection of Australian art in the world.

The gallery curates three permanent collections – the **Western**, **Australian** and **Asian Galleries**. The **Archibald Prize** for Australian portraiture is unfailingly controversial and exhibits here annually, as do the Wynne Prize (landscape or figure sculpture) and Sulman Prize (subject or mural painting) exhibitions and the **Artexpress** exhibition of the year's best HSC student art. Kids swarm to **Sunday Fundays** (p36) which offer workshops, performances and free guided tours with costumed actors. There are also concerts, screenings, courses, celebrity talks and programs for deaf and visually impaired people. Grab a coffee in a terrace café or restaurant and channel your inspiration.

PADDINGTON & SURROUNDS (6, D4)

Paddington, aka 'Paddo', 4km east of the CBD, is an elegant, expensive area of restored terrace houses and steep leafy streets. Rugged bushland until the 1860s, Paddington was built for aspiring Victorian artisans, but after the lemming-like rush to outer suburban quarter-acre blocks post-WWII, Paddington became Australia's worst slum. A renewed passion for Victorian architecture and the alarming realisation that the outer suburbs were unspeakably boring led to Paddington's resurgence in the 1960s. By the '90s, real estate was out of reach for all but the lucky and the loaded.

In Paddington today there's a desperately fashionable waft between meticulously restored terraces, designer shops, chic restaurants, art galleries and bookshops. The pulsing lifeblood of Paddington and

INFORMATION
🚌 352, 378, 380, 389, L82
✂ p77

Oxford St: pretty in pink

nearby Darlinghurst is **Oxford St**. The street's flamboyant spirit comes courtesy of its vibrant gay community – the **Sydney Gay & Lesbian Mardi Gras** (p92) parade gyrates through here every February. **Taylor Square** (6, B4) is gay Sydney's decadent nucleus.

Explore Paddington's streets and hibiscus-lined laneways any time (walking tour p40), although it's best on Saturdays when the **Paddington Bazaar** (p49) is pumping. Join the meandering market throngs – indulge in a foot massage, tarot reading or funky shirt to wear clubbing that night.

At the eastern end of Oxford St is **Centennial Park** (6, E6), Sydney's biggest park. It's a grassy 220-hectare expanse filled with people walking, kicking balls around, cycling, rollerblading, horse-riding or relaxing under a trees with books. During summer, **Moonlight Cinema** (p87), classical music concerts and dance parties rustle the foliage.

DON'T MISS
- Feisty frocked-up frolickers at the **Gay & Lesbian Mardi Gras** (p92).
- A schooner of local lager or three in an Art Deco Paddo pub (p77).
- Chuckle smugly and hobnob with the rich elite in Paddington's galleries (p29) and Woollahra's antique shops (p59).
- Café coffee at **Five Ways** (p77).

Man, this codpiece is tight...

MANLY (4)

Laid-back Manly clings to a narrow isthmus near **North Head** (2, F2). Between ocean and harbour beaches, Manly contrasts resort trappings with community sensibilities. Shaggy surfers, dusty labourers, sunburnt backpackers and relaxed locals make a refreshing change from the stuffy, moneyed harbour enclaves nearby.

Riding the Manly Ferry is a great way to fathom Sydney Harbour. The half-hour trip chugs east from Circular Quay (15min by JetCat).

The **Corso** (4, B2) connects Manly's ocean and harbour beaches – surf shops, burger joints, juice bars and lousy cappuccino cafés proliferate. The refurbished **Manly Wharf** (4, A2) has classier cafés, pubs and restaurants. West of here is the sharky aquarium **Oceanworld** (p28) and the beachy **Manly Art Gallery & Museum** (4, A2; ☎ 9949 1776; $3.50/1.10; ✆ 10am-5pm Tue-Sun).

INFORMATION

- 🖳 www.manlytourism .com
- ℹ Manly Visitors Information Centre (☎ 9977 1088; ✆ 9am-5pm Mon-Fri, 10am-4pm Sat & Sun)
- 🚢 Manly
- 🚌 151, 169, E69 from Wynyard Park
- ✗ μ78

North Head Scenic Drive (4, B3) provides stunning ocean, harbour and city views. Nearby, **North Fort** (2, F2; ☎ 9976 6102, www.northfort.org .au, North Head Scenic Dr; $8/5/15; ✆ 11am-4pm Wed, Sat & Sun) houses the Royal Australian Artillery National Museum. **Manly Quarantine Station** (2, F2; ☎ 9247 5033; North Head Scenic Dr; $11/7.50; ✆ 1.15pm Tue, Thu, Sat & Sun, bookings essential) isolated epidemic disease carriers between 1832 and 1984. Ghosts of the dead linger; take the **Ghost Tour** ($27.50/22; ✆ 8pm Fri-Sun) or kids' **Junior Ghostbusters Tour** (p37).

Manly hosts a Food and Wine Festival in June, an Arts Festival in September and an International Jazz Festival in October. Sydney Rd has a **weekend craft market**. The amazingly varied 10km **Manly Scenic Walkway** (p41) tracks west towards The Spit Bridge – the perfect afternoon escape.

Enter Sandmen

Manly was one of the first places in Australia to be given a European moniker – history suggests Captain Phillip named the beach after the 'manly' physiques of the Aborigines he met on the sand here in 1788. Perpetuating this reputation today are the bronzed bodysurfing battalions who out-testosterone each other in the breaks. Head for protected **Shelly Beach** (4, C2) if you're feeling inadequate.

TARONGA ZOO (2, D3)

Haven't spotted any kangaroos bounding down George St yet? A 15-minute ferry ride from Circular Quay, Taronga Zoo has 75 hectares of bushy harbour hillside chock-full of kangaroos, koalas and similarly hirsute Australians. The zoo's 4000 critters have million-dollar views but seem blissfully unaware of the privilege.

The **platypus habitat** is a favourite – day and night have been switched to let you see nocturnal platypuses in action. Go snap-happy at the **koala display**, or book a wander with kangaroos and wallabies at the **Australian Walkabout** (they'll acknowledge your intrusion with a yawn). **Backyard to Bush** lets kids (big and small) get close to farm animals with interpretive displays.

Animals are more animated in the morning and late afternoon, especially on hot days, and you're more likely to dodge annoying tour groups if you visit then. The zoo is really steep so work your way down from the top if you're leaving by ferry. Can't be bothered walking to the top entrance from the ferry when you arrive? Take the **Sky Safari** cable car (included in admission) or a bus.

Roar & Snore (☎ 9969 2777; $88; ☽ Fri & Sat nights) is a fun

INFORMATION

- ☎ 9969 2777
- 🖥 www.zoo.nsw.gov.au
- ✉ Bradleys Head Rd, Mosman
- 💲 25/17.50; ZooPass from Circular Quay includes return ferry rides, admission & Sky Safari ($31.70/15.40)
- ☽ 9am-5pm (last admission 4.30pm)
- ℹ feeding shows and keeper talks throughout the day; twilight concerts Feb-Mar; baby strollers for hire
- 🚢 from Circular Quay
- 🚌 247
- 🅿 $10
- ♿ good (including access from ferry; zoo maps show access; wheelchairs for hire)
- 🍴 Zoo café

Ooo ooo ooo aah aah aah

DON'T MISS

- The **giraffe enclosure** with views to the Harbour Bridge and Opera House.
- The raucous **seal show** (☽ 1pm).
- Twilight **summer concerts**: finger-snappin' jazz, over-the-top opera and composed classical.

overnight family experience with a night-time zoo safari, barbeque dinner and tents pitched under the stars. Breakfast and a behind-the-scenes tour arrive with the dawn.

Taronga has an important endangered species breeding program, successes with Sumatran tigers, red pandas, orang-utans and snow leopards. The **Asian Elephant Rainforest** opens late 2004, with **Great Southern Oceans** following in 2005.

VAUCLUSE HOUSE   (2, E3)

Sydney's last remaining 19th-century harbourside estate, Vaucluse House (1828) is an imposing, turreted specimen of Gothic Australiana set among 10 hectares of lush gardens. Decorated with beautiful European period pieces including Bohemian glass, heavy oak 'Jacobethan' furniture and Meissen china, the house offers visitors a rare glimpse into early (albeit privileged) colonial life in Sydney. Also featured are stables, tea rooms and a separate kitchen block with its own garden.

INFORMATION

☎ 9388 7922

🖥 www.hht.net.au

✉ Wentworth Rd, Vaucluse

$ 7/3/17

🕑 10am-4.30pm Tue-Sun

🚍 325

P free on site

♿ ground floor only

✗ tea rooms

Vaucluse House was built and occupied by **William Charles Wentworth**, his wife Sarah and their children from 1827–62. The son of a convict mother, Wentworth became a barrister and co-wrote the first NSW colonial constitution but was outcast from high society because of his democratic leanings. He held the 'outrageous' view that Australian-born colonials were the equals of the English, and that political and legal rights should be extended to emancipists (freed convicts). Wentworth is also famous for his bold explorations with Blaxland and Lawson (see below).

If in need of a swim, the Wentworths would no doubt have strolled down to the beach at **Shark Bay** (p33) in **Nielsen Park**, once part of the then 206-hectare Vaucluse House estate. Today it's surrounded by a section of the Sydney Harbour National Park and is one of the harbour's best family beaches, its waters protected from namesake sharks by netting.

Afternoon tea with the Wentworths

Wandering Will Wentworth

William Charles Wentworth – patriot, legal maestro, astute politician, social agitator – was also an avid explorer. In 1813, he, Blaxland and Lawson were the first Europeans to traverse the Blue Mountains. Today's Western Highway follows their route, winding through the sleepy mountain towns of Blaxland, Lawson and Wentworth Falls. **Wentworth Falls** themselves are breathtaking – visit after rains if possible. Just past Katoomba, the trio notched the **Explorers' Tree** to mark their trail. Under a derelict pagoda, this sad bushfire-ravaged stump has been amputated, gored by termites and filled with concrete to stop it collapsing, earning it the title *Eucalyptus concretus*.

Sights & Activities

MUSEUMS & NOTABLE BUILDINGS

Anzac Memorial (5, D8)
The interior dome of this dignified Art Deco memorial is studded with one star for each of the 120,000 NSW citizens who served in WWI. The pines near the entrance grew from seeds gathered at Gallipoli; the Pool of Remembrance and *Sacrifice* sculpture are particularly poignant.
☎ 9267 7668 ☐ www .rslnsw.com.au ✉ Hyde Park ⑤ free ⊙ 9am-5pm ⑱ Museum Ⓜ World Square ♿ ground floor only

Australian Museum (5, E7)
Established only 40 years after the First Fleet dropped anchor, this natural history museum has excellent Aboriginal and native wildlife exhibitions. There are self-guided tours, indigenous dance and didgeridoo performances on Sundays and kids get busy in the Dinosaur, Skeleton and Search & Discover galleries.
☎ 9320 6000 ☐ www .amonline.net.au ✉ 6-8 College St ⑤ 8/4/19 ⊙ 9.30am-5pm ⑱ Museum Ⓜ Galeries Victoria Ⓟ discount with museum admission ♿ excellent (via College St)

Customs House (5, D4)
By the time you read this, wholesale renovations to this cavernous harbourside construction will be complete. The grand old building (1885) contains the Sydney Exhibition Space and its charmingly geeky 1:500 model of Sydney. The slick **Cafe Sydney**

(p68) has jazz and sweeping harbour views.
☎ 9247 2285 ☐ www .customshouse.com.au ✉ 31 Alfred St ⑤ free ⊙ 10am-5pm ⑱ ⑱ ⑳ Circular Quay ♿ good

Elizabeth Bay House (6, C2) Built between 1835 and 1839 for Colonial Secretary Alexander Macleay, this elegant neoclassical mansion was once the finest house in the colony, its grounds extending to Kings Cross. Ugly 20th-century apartments now surround it, but the exquisitely engineered oval salon and stairwell are timeless in architectural delight.
☎ 9356 3022 ☐ www .hht.net.au ✉ 7 Onslow Ave, Elizabeth Bay ⑤ 7/3/17 ⊙ 10am-4.30pm Tue-Sun ⑱ Kings Cross ⑱ 311 ♿ ground floor only, car space

Hyde Park Barracks Museum (5, E6) Designed by prolific convict architect Francis Greenway, the

barracks were convict quarters for Anglo-Irish sinners (1819–48), an immigrant depot/asylum (1848–86) and government courts/offices (1887–1979) before its current incarnation – a window into everyday convict life. There's also a bookshop and café.
☎ 9223 8922 ☐ www .hht.net.au ✉ Queens Sq ⑤ 7/3/17, free courtyard & introductory room ⊙ 9.30am-5pm ⑱ St James Ⓜ City Centre ♿ ground floor only

Justice & Police Museum (5, E4) In the old Water Police Station (1856), this museum adopts the guise of a late-19th-century police station and court. Exhibits focus on various disreputable activities, including forensic evidence from Sydney's most heinous crimes, weapons, drug busts and lots of butt-ugly mugshots only a mother could love.
☎ 9252 1144 ☐ www .hht.net.au ✉ cnr Albert & Phillip Sts ⑤ 7/3/17

Rum Hospital History
Sydney's **Parliament House** (p27) and **Mint** (5, E6) are twin buildings, the former wings of the infamous Rum Hospital, so-called because its builders' payment took the form of a lucrative three-year monopoly on rum sales. Due to appalling medical practices and lax patient treatment, no one was sad to see the hospital's main building razed and **Sydney Hospital** built on the site in 1894. Rubbing the snout of the **Little Boar** statue out the front and lobbing coins in the donation box brings good luck (and might just keep you out of hospital).

🕙 10am-5pm Sat &
Sun, daily in Jan, group
bookings Mon-Fri
🚆 🚌 🚢 Circular Quay
♿ ground floor only

Museum of Contemporary Art (5, D3) In a
harbourside Art Deco edifice,
the Museum of Contemporary Art has been raising
even the most open-minded
Sydney eyebrows since it
opened in 1991. Constantly
changing controversial exhibitions from Australia and
overseas range from incredibly hip and self-indulgent
to in-your-face, sexually
explicit and profoundly
disturbing. Dig it.
☎ 9252 4033
🖥 www.mca.com.au
✉ 140 George St
💲 free 🕙 10am-5pm
🚆 🚌 🚢 Circular Quay
♿ good (via George St)

Museum of Sydney (5, D4)
Built where Sydney's first
and infamously pungent
Government House once
stood, this layered, tale-weaving museum uses
state-of-the-art installations to explore the city's
people, places, cultures and
evolution over two centuries, honouring indigenous
origins and tracing the city's
mellifluous physical form.
☎ 9251 5988 🖥 www
.hht.net.au ✉ cnr Bridge
& Phillip Sts 💲 7/3/17
🕙 9.30am-5pm
🚆 🚌 🚢 Circular Quay
♿ ground floor only

Parliament House (5, E5)
deep veranda, formal
shade and ochre tones
noble building
ark back to colonial

Say, 'Ahhh...' at the Australian Museum

days. It's the world's oldest
continuously operating
parliamentary building –
inside you'll find art
exhibitions and a display on
government structure. The
public gallery opens on days
when Parliament sits.
☎ 9230 2111 🖥 www
.parliament.nsw.gov.au
✉ Macquarie St 💲 free
🕙 9.30am-4pm Mon-Fri
🚆 Martin Place
♿ excellent

**Powerhouse Museum
(5, B8)** Sydney's hippest
and most progressive
museum whirrs away inside
an enormous building,
once the power station
for Sydney's defunct tram
network. This is the place
for the low-down on how
lightning strikes, magnets
grab or engines growl.
Visitors surge through doors
for high-voltage interaction,
education, experiments and
demonstrations.
☎ 9217 0111 🖥 www
.phm.gov.au ✉ 500 Harris St, Ultimo 💲 10/5/23,
special exhibits extra
🕙 10am-5pm Ⓜ Powerhouse Museum 🚆 Hay-

market 🚌 501 from
Town Hall ♿ excellent

St James Church (5, E6)
Constructed from convict
bricks, Sydney's oldest
church (1819) is another
Francis Greenway extravaganza. Originally designed
as a courthouse, the brief
changed: 'Hey Frank, we
need a church!' The cells
became the crypt. Check out
the balcony, sparking copper dome above the altar
and the cool contemporary
stained-glass 'Creation
Window'.
☎ 9232 3022 🖥 www
.stjameschurchsydney
.org.au ✉ Queens Sq
💲 free 🕙 8am-5pm
Mon-Sat, 7.30am-4pm
Sun; free guided tours
2.30pm Mon-Fri 🚆 St
James Ⓜ City Centre

St Mary's Cathedral (5, E6)
Built to last, this Gothic
megalith is one of the
world's largest cathedrals.
The first service was held
here in 1833, but the massive spires weren't finished
until 2000. The crypt's
mosaic floor depicting the

Creation was inspired by the *Book of Kells*.
☎ 9220 0400 🖳 www.sydney.catholic.org.au ✉ cnr College St & St Marys Rd 💲 free 🕒 6.30am-6.30pm Sun-Fri, 7am-7pm Sat; mass daily, confession Mon-Sat, devotions Fri 🚊 St James ♿ fair

Sydney Jewish Museum
(6, B3) Created as a living memorial to the Holocaust, the Sydney Jewish Museum examines Australian Jewish history, culture and tradition from the time of the First Fleet to the present day.
☎ 9331 4245 🖳 www.sydneyjewishmuseum.com.au ✉ 148 Darlinghurst Rd 💲 10/7/22 🕒 10am-4pm Sun-Thu, to 2pm Fri, closed Jewish holidays 🚊 Kings Cross 🚌 311, 389

Victoria Barracks (6, C5)
A manicured malarial vision from the peak of the British Empire, these Georgian buildings have been called the finest in the colonies. Thursday's tours include a flag-raising ceremony, marching band (subject to

---

Timely Museum Pass
The Heritage Housing Trusts's **Ticket Through Time** (☎ 9692 8366; www.hht.net.au/visit/admissions; $23/10/40) gets you into all 11 of the HHT's houses and museums in the Sydney area, including Vaucluse House (p25), Government House (p17), Elizabeth Bay House (p26), Justice & Police Museum (p26), Museum of Sydney (p27), Hyde Park Barracks Museum (p26) and Susannah Place (p14). Visit four or more of these and you'll save yourself some hard-earned cash.

---

availability) and a squiz at the paraphernalia-packed war museum.
☎ 9339 3170 ✉ cnr Oxford St & Greens Rd, Paddington (entry opposite Shadforth St) 💲 2 for museum 🕒 tour 10am-12.30pm Thu, museum 10am-3pm Sun, closed Dec-Feb 🚌 325, 378, 380, L82 ♿ good

OCEANIA

Australian National Maritime Museum (5, B6)
Beneath an Utzon-like roof, the Maritime Museum sails through Australia's inextricable relationship with the sea. Exhibitions range from Aboriginal canoes to the First Fleet to surf culture and the Navy. You can almost taste the sea salt.
☎ 9298 3777 🖳 www.anmm.gov.au ✉ Darling Harbour 💲 10/6/25 special exhibits extra 🕒 9.30am-5pm (to 6pm Jan) 🚊 Town Hall Ⓜ Harbourside 🚊 🚢 Pyrmont Bay ♿ good (not to ships) Ⓟ discount at Harbourside

Oceanworld (4, A2) This ain't the place to come if you're on the way to Manly Beach for a surf. Inside this daggy-looking '80s building are underwater glass tubes through which you become alarmingly intimate with sting rays and 10ft sharks. Reckon they're not hungry?
Shark Dive Extreme ($195/150 introductory/certified) takes you into their world…
☎ 9949 2644 🖳 www.oceanworld.com.au ✉ West Esplanade, Manly 💲 16.50/12 🕒 10am-5.30pm (last admission 4.45pm) 🚢 Manly 🚌 151, 169, E69 from Wynyard Park

Sydney Aquarium (5, C6)
A seemingly endless tide of visitors flows through the Sydney Aquarium. The bait? 160m of underwater tunnels and 11,000 Australian sea animals. Swoon over Van Gogh colours in the Great Barrier Reef exhibit or shudder with Darwinian revulsion as humungous sharks pass an inch from your face in the Open Ocean exhibit.
☎ 9262 2300 🖳 www.sydneyaquarium.com.au ✉ Darling Harbour 💲 24 16/family deals 🕒 9am-10pm (last admission 9p 🚊 Town Hall Ⓜ Dar' Park 🚢 Darling Harb Ⓟ discount at Harb side ♿ excellent

GALLERIES

Galleries play a pivotal role in Sydney's visual arts scene; a tense, competitive vibe runs between Paddington, Surry Hills/Redfern and CBD galleries. See 'Arts & Exhibitions' in the Metro section of Friday's *Sydney Morning Herald* ($1.20) and the monthly *Art Almanac* ($3) for listings. Many galleries close through Christmas/January and on Mondays. Galleries below are free unless otherwise indicated.

Art Gallery of NSW (5, F6) See p21.

Artspace (6, B1) Artspace is spacey; their eternal quest is to fill the void with vigorous, engaging Australian and international contemporary art. Things are avant-garde — expect lots of conceptual pieces, video and sound installations and new-media masterpieces. ☎ 9368 1899 ⌨ www .artspace.org.au ✉ The Gunnery, 43-51 Cowper Wharf Rdwy, Woolloomooloo ⌚ 11am-5pm Tue-Sat ⓡ Kings Cross ⌑ 311 ♿ good

Asia-Australian Arts Centre (5, C9) Opened with glee by Lord Mayor Frank Sartor in 2000, this vibrant, cross-culturally fused gallery exhibits the best of living Asian arts in Australia. Politicians continue to turn up and cut ribbons for director Binghui Huangfu, gaining maximum exposure for nonprofit calligraphic installations and photographic displays. ☎ 9212 0380 ⌨ info@4a.com.au ✉ 181-7 Hay St ⌚ 11am-6pm Tue-Sat ⓡ Central Ⓜ Power-house Museum ⓡ Capi-tare ⌑ George St ground floor

Australian Centre for Photography (6, D5) The non-profit ACP exhibits the photographic gems of renowned Sydney and international photographers on a five-to-six-week rotation, while its 'Project Wall' highlights new artists. They get particularly passionate about photomedia and digital imaging works. After you've gone snap-happy, focus in on the bookshop and **Bistro Lulu** (p77). ☎ 9332 1455 ⌨ www .acp.au.com ✉ 257 Oxford St, Paddington ⌚ 11am-6pm ⌑ 325, 378, 380, L82

Australian Galleries (6, E4) Contemporary Australian painting and sculpture for Paddo's cashed-up collectors. The A-list of artists includes David Allen, Peter Doyle, Lloyd Rees and Jeffrey Smart. Works on paper feature at the

Glenmore Rd branch (6, C4; ☎ 9380 8744; 24 Glenmore Rd; ⌚ 10am-6pm Tue-Sat, noon-5pm Sun). ☎ 9360 5177 ⌨ www .australiangalleries.com .au ✉ 15 Roylston St, Paddington ⌚ 10am-6pm Mon-Sat ⌑ 325, 378, 380, 389, L82

Brett Whiteley Studio (6, A6) Whiteley was rock 'n' roll artistry — he lived fast and without restraint, and when he fired up and let fly on the canvass, everybody went '*Ooohh!*' His studio has been preserved as a gallery for some of his best work. Get in early for weekend discussions, performances, readings and workshops. ☎ 9225 1881 ⌨ www .brettwhiteley.org ✉ 2 Raper St, Surry Hills 💲 7/5 ⌚ 10am-4pm Sat & Sun ⓡ ⓡ Central ⌑ 301-3, 343, 372 ♿ fair

Brett Whiteley Studio — a life less ordinary

Things can get weird at the Museum of Contemporary Art

Gould Galleries (6, E5) Got a spare 80 grand? Swank in and bang your wad on the counter. It's guaranteed to proffer timeless works by big-name 20th-century Australian painters. Expect canvases by bankable heavyweights like Arthur Boyd, Sidney Nolan, Brett Whiteley, Margaret Preston and Charles Blackburn.
☎ 9328 9222 🖳 www .gouldgalleries.com ✉ 110 Queen St, Woollahra 🕑 11am-6pm Mon-Fri, to 5pm Sat, 2-5pm Sun 🚌 325, 378, 380, 389, L82

Museum of Contemporary Art (5, D3)
See p27.

Ray Hughes Gallery (6, A6) Beyond the corrugated iron cows and 1920s vending machines, old-time art dealer Ray Hughes wheels and deals. The Australian, Aboriginal and Pacific art he flogs is some of Australia's classiest. Even if you don't buy a cow, his bohemian warehouse is worth a look.
☎ 9698 3200; fax 9699 2796 ✉ 270 Devonshire St, Surry Hills 🕑 10am-6pm Tue-Sat 🚉 🚉 Central 🚌 301

SH Ervin Gallery (5, C4) High on the hill, this popular art museum presents changing exhibitions (six-to-eight-week rotation) of historical and contemporary Australian art. Annual exhibitions include the *Salon des Refuses* (an alternative selection of Archibald Prize entries), *The Year in Art* and the *Portia Geach Memorial Award*.
☎ 9258 0173 🖳 www .nsw.nationaltrust.org .au/ervin.html ✉ National Trust Centre, Observatory Park, Watsons Rd, The Rocks 💲 6/4 🕑 11am-5pm Tue-Fri, noon-5pm Sat & Sun 🚉 Circular Quay, Wynyard 🚌 339, 431-4 ⛴ Circular Quay ♿ good

Sherman Galleries (6, D4) Big-time Australian artists command big-time prices inside this schmick architect-designed sculpture and contemporary art salon. Polished concrete floors, spot-lit white walls and a sculpture garden make the prospect of owning something by Imants Tillers, Michael Johnson, Anne Graham or Janet Lawrence seem oddly attainable.
☎ 9331 1112 🖳 www .shermangalleries.com.au

✉ 16-18 Goodhope St, Paddington 🕑 10am-6pm Tue-Fri, 11am-6pm Sat 🚌 325, 378, 380, 389, L82 ♿ good

Stills Gallery (6, C3) In the slick innards of a former film studio, Stills specialises in contemporary Australian photography and photo-media-based art. Exhibits range from photomontage to B&W documentary photography to large-scale conceptual colour and digital image making.
☎ 9331 7775 🖳 www .stillsgallery.com.au ✉ 36 Gosbell St, Paddington 🕑 11am-6pm Wed-Sat, by appointment Tue 🚌 325, 378, 380, 389, L82 ♿ fair

Wagner Art Gallery (6, D4) Think Boyd, Lindsay, Nolan and Friend. Think top dollar. Think champagne, turtlenecked, lah-de-dah openings (🕑 6-8pm one Tue/month). Wagner is one of the oldest galleries in Paddington, its maturity reflected in its composed atmosphere and high-brow decency.
☎ 9360 6069 🖳 www .wagnerartgallery.com.au ✉ 39 Gurner St, Paddington 🕑 10.30am-6pm Mon-Sat, 1-6pm Sun 🚌 325, 378, 380, 389, L82

Watters Gallery (6, A3) This funky institution (since 1964) in the seamy lower reaches of Riley St keeps pumping out quality; James Gleeson, Ken Whisson, R Klippel, Richard Larter reformed rock star Mombassa are ju

of the Australian art icons it holds up to the light.
☎ 9331 2556 🖥 www.wattersgallery.com ✉ 109 Riley St, East Sydney 🕑 10am-5pm Tue, to 7pm Wed-Fri 🚇 Museum 🚌 389

Indigenous Art

Aboriginal & Tribal Art Centre (5, D3) Follow the rainbow serpent mural upstairs to this scrupulously authentic gallery exhibiting works by central desert, Arnhem Land and Bathurst Island artists. It's one of the few galleries to stock Tiwi-designed fabrics, pandanus weavings and emu-feather baskets. Important artists Roy Burrunyula and Djardie Ashley regularly exhibit.
☎ 9247 9625 🖥 www.aboriginalandtribalart.com ✉ L1 117 George St, the Rocks 🕑 10am-5.30pm (to 5pm Sun) 🚌 🚌 🚢 Circular Quay

Australian Art Print Network (6, A3) Lustrous screen prints, rare limited editions and quality lithographs, etchings and linocuts make this subterranean gallery a stand out. It houses Sydney's most expansive collection of prints by Australia's leading indigenous artists; look for works by Dennis Nona, Rover Thomas and Queenie McKenzie.
☎ 9332 1722 🖥 www.aboriginalartprints.com.au ✉ LG 68 Oxford St, Darlinghurst 🕑 9am-6pm Mon-Fri, 11am-5pm Sat, by appointment Sun 🚌 325, 378, 380, L82

Black Fella's Dreaming (6, B4) Founded by noted indigenous artist Gordon Syron, this place is an ethereal, cutting-edge Aboriginal-owned gallery supporting Aboriginal people in the selling, promotion, curation and documentation of their art. Exhibits are challenging, progressive and powerful, created with a strong spirit of self-determination and respect.
☎ 9331 8701 🖥 www.blackfellasdreaming.com.au ✉ 239 Oxford St, Darlinghurst 🕑 11am-7pm Mon-Fri, to 9pm Sat & Sun 🚌 325, 378, 380, L82

Gavala (5, B7) Selling only authentic Aboriginal products that are licensed, authorised or purchased directly from artists or communities, Gavala stirs up an outback vibe and has a mind-boggling array of paintings, hunting boomerangs, didgeridoos, handmade artefacts, books, clothing, CDs and tapes.
☎ 9212 7232 🖥 www.gavala.com.au ✉ Shop 131, L1 Harbourside 🕑 10am-9pm 🚇 Town Hall Ⓜ 🚢 Convention 🚢 Pyrmont Bay Ⓟ Harbourside ♿ fair

Hogarth Galleries (6, C4) A cultural beacon in an obscure Paddington laneway, Hogarth has supported and promoted Aboriginal art since 1972. Honouring established artists and sourcing up-and-comers, Hogarth exhibits contemporary dot paintings, basketry, framed prints, fabrics, spears and didgeridoos.
☎ 9360 6839 🖥 www.aboriginalartcentres.com ✉ 7 Walker La, Paddington 🕑 10am-5pm Tue-Sat 🚌 325, 378, 380, L82

Buying Indigenous Art

Over the past 20 years, Aboriginal art has soared to global popularity. Traditional methods and spiritual significance are fastidiously maintained, but have found a counterpart in Western materials – the results can be wildly original interpretations of traditional stories and ceremonial designs.

Much traditional and contemporary indigenous art available in galleries and shops comes from elsewhere Australia, and can cost anywhere from $200 to ,000. Make sure you're buying art from an authentic aler, artist or community and not perpetuating digenous cash-in on Aboriginal art's popularity.

BEACHES

Sydney's beaches teem with weekend life, but locals often swim before, after or instead of going to work. Most are easily accessible, clean and are patrolled by surf lifesavers. Shark patrols operate during the summer. Don't panic, Sydney has only had one fatal shark attack since 1937, and dorsal-fin sightings are rare enough to make the nightly news. Many beaches are topless; a couple are nude – do as the locals do.

Avalon (1, E1) Caught up in a sandy '70s time-warp, Avalon is the mythical Australian beach you always dreamed was there but never managed to find. The surf's consistent, and the re-laxed back streets are lined with sleepy cafés, second-hand bookshops and even a small cinema. See **Northern Beaches** p43.
🚌 L88, L90

Balmoral (2, E2) Split into two sections by an unfeasibly quaint rocky outcrop, Balmoral is popular with picnicking North Shore families. Swimmers, kayakers, windsurfers and dragon-boat racers migrate to the shark-netted southern end. Don't miss the Spanish Mission–style **Bathers' Pavilion** (p78) for lunch or dinner.

🚌 275 from Spit Junction, 328 from Taronga Zoo

Bondi (Map 3)
See p9; restaurants p64.

Bronte (2, E5) Norfolk Island pines and sandstone headlands hem in the bowl-shaped park behind Bronte, a small family-oriented beach that can get wild and sea-weedy on a stormy day. The rock pool is one of the best, as are the dozen beachy cafés (p64) which have populated the once exceedingly uncool shopping strip.
🚌 378

Camp Cove (2, E3) When Phillip realised Botany Bay just didn't cut it he sailed north into Sydney Harbour, his boots sinking into Camp Cove's sand on 21 January 1788. It's a gorgeous golden harbour beach frequented by rich Watsons Bay families, topless beach babes and photo-manic tourists.
🚉 Watsons Bay
🚌 324-5, L24, L82 from Bondi Junction

Clovelly (2, E6) The concrete terrace around the mouth of this long, skinny bay makes Clovelly more pool than beach, but the swell still surges in. A beloved friendly groper fish lived here for many years until he was speared by a tourist a few years ago. Bring your mask and snorkel, but don't even think about killing anything.
🚌 339 ♿ disabled ramp into water

Coogee (2, E6) Coogee is an Aboriginal word for malo-dorous rotting seaweed, but don't let that put you off. The

All on the same wavelength – surf's up at Bondi

beach is wide; plenty of room for pallid frisbee-throwing backpackers, surf grommets and groovers alike. If it's stormy, pull up a stool and a schooner in the **Coogee Bay Hotel** (p81) and watch Neptune's fury.

🚌 372-4, X73-4, 313-4 & 353 from Bondi Junction

Cronulla (1, E3) Cronulla's *looong* beach stretches beyond the dunes to the Botany Bay oil refineries and airport flight path. It's an edgy place, with dingy fish-and-chip shops, insomnious teens and a ragged air of impending 'something'. Gabrielle Carey and Kathy Lette captured this sense in their '70s cult Cronulla teen novel *Puberty Blues*.

🚉 Cronulla

Dee Why (1, E2) Curiously distorted from *diwai*, an Aboriginal name for a local bird, Dee Why sees grommets hitting the waves and mums hitting the rock pool. It's a no-fuss family beach fronted by chunky apartments, some good cafés and ubiquitous surf shops. See **Northern Beaches** (p43).

🚌 136

Lady Bay (2, E3) Sometimes called Lady Jane Bay, this diminutive, mainly gay nudist beach sits at the bottom of a cliff, on top of which (somewhat ironically) is a sprawling Royal Australian Navy facility. To get here, ~~w~~ the cliff-top walking ~~from~~ (somewhat ironi-~~mp~~ Cove.

~~h~~ Head 🚌 324-~~ from Bondi

Nude Ain't Rude

Victorian conservatism banned daylight bathing in Sydney until 1903 (the beaches must have been kickin' at night). In 1907, a law was passed permitting neck-to-knee swimming costumes only; beach inspectors patrolled the sands with tape measures ejecting the ribald and indiscreet. By 1930, hems were on the rise and it was only a matter of time before nude was rude no more. These days, Sydney's beaches seethe with as much skin as sand.

Manly (Map 4) See p23.

Maroubra (1, E3) Maroubra rivals Bondi for size and swell, but its suburban location renders it immune to the more refined trappings of Sydney's most famous beach. The notorious 'Bra Boys' gang remains entrenched in the psyche of the community, but don't let their presence stop you enjoying the surf.

🚌 376-7, 395-6, X77, X96

Palm Beach (1, E1) The northernmost of the Northern Beaches, Palm Beach is a meniscus of bliss. Barrenjoey Lighthouse overlooks the windswept northern end where nudists roam free. At the more sheltered southern end, the cast and crew from inexplicably enduring Australian TV soap *Home & Away* film their treacle-plot episodes. See **Northern Beaches** (p43).

🚌 L90, 190, 193 from Avalon

Shark Beach (2, E3) Despite the name, there's really nothing to worry about – a shark net protects swimmers from becoming something's lunch. It's a family scene, with a super harbour outlook and the shady, subtly spooky Nielsen Park as a backdrop.

✉ Nielsen Park, Vaucluse 🚌 325

Tamarama (3, B3) Tamarama, set in a deep sexy gulch with models and generically gorgeous aplenty, fully deserves its nickname 'Glamarama'. Signs say 'no frisbees, no kites, no ball games'. No fun. Still, if you feel at home here, you're probably not into those kinds of things anyway...

🚌 361

Tamarama/Glamarama

OUTDOOR STUFF

Dawn Fraser Baths (2, B3)

If Balmain's endless photogenia doesn't float your boat, head to Elkington Park. The magnificently restored late-Victorian timber enclosure at the tidal Dawn Fraser Baths (1884) picturesquely protects swimmers from underwater undesirables. Australia's all-conquering 1956–64 Olympian Dawn Fraser sacrificed her youth here swimming laps.
☎ 9555 1903 ✉ Elkington Park, Glassop St, Balmain 💲 3.20/2.10 🕑 7.15am-5.30pm Mar-Nov, 6.45am-7pm Dec-Feb 🚌 431-4, 441-2, 445-6

Featherdale Wildlife Park (1, C2)

Over 2000 Australian native beasts live here in a natural bush setting, eating, sleeping, shagging, defecating and doing all that good beastly stuff. Hand-feed kangaroos, wallabies and emus, slither through the reptile pavilion, stroke a soporific koala or kill some time with a dingo or a Tasmanian devil (no, they don't spin around like tornados).
☎ 9622 1644 🖥 www.featherdale.com.au

✉ 217-29 Kildare Rd, Doonside 💲 16.50/13/42 🕑 9am-5pm 🚉 Blacktown then 🚌 725 🚗 40min from Sydney ♿ excellent 🅿 free

Harbour Jet (5, B7)

The Harbour Jet boats (more akin to rockets) propel you around the harbour in an untamed, white-knuckle, sea-spray ride of 270° spins, fish-tails and 75km/h power-brake stops that'll test how long it's been since you had breakfast.
☎ 1300 887 373 🖥 www.harbourjet.com ✉ Shop 113a, L1 Harbourside 💲 60/35/135 🕑 9am-9pm 🚉 Town Hall Ⓜ 🚌 Convention 🚢 Pyrmont Bay

Let's Go Surfing (3, C1)

Always wanted to join the tribe of rubber-people bobbing around in the Bondi waves? Here's your chance: two-hour lessons including board and wetsuit hire are $59/49 – paddle out the back, wait for a fat set and get radical dude. Prefer Manly? Try **Manly Surf School** (4, B1; ☎ 9977 6977; www.manlysurf

school.com; North Steyne Beach).
☎ 9365 1800 🖥 www.letsgosurfing.com.au ✉ 128 Ramsgate Ave, Bondi Beach 💲 25/2hr surfboard & wetsuit hire (no instruction) 🕑 9am-7pm 🚌 380, 389, L82 from Circular Quay, 381-2 from Bondi Junction

Rollerblading Sydney (2, C3)

Crossing the Sydney Harbour Bridge by car is so passé... Get some wheels on your heels. Reassuringly proficient rollerblade instructor James O'Conner will get you barrelling across the 'old coat hanger' with lessons, quality skates and protective gear.
☎ 0411 872 022 🖥 www.rollerbladingsydney.com.au ✉ Milsons Point train station 💲 55/1hr, 99/2hr 🕑 8am-6pm Mon-Fri, 9am-7pm Sat & Sun 🚉 Milsons Point

Simply Skydive (5, D6)

Hysteria defined: strap yourself to the chest of a complete stranger then hurl yourself from an aeroplane 14,000ft up without oxygen. If you remember to look during your 60-second freefall, there'll be unbelievable views of Sydney and the Blue Mountains.
☎ 1800 759 3483 🖥 www.simplyskydive.com.au ✉ Shop CM12 Mezzanine Level, Centrepoint, Pitt St Mall 💲 275 midweek specials 🕑 daily pick-up from C

You punch the shark on the nose, like this... Works every time mate.

Sydney Rock Pools

Sydneysiders aren't always desperate to hurl themselves into the Pacific. Sometimes they just want to swim a few salty laps without the difficulties imposed by malicious dumpers and ocean dwellers. So inclined, they head for the protected tidal pools built below the cliffs at rocky beach-ends. From north to south, the following beaches have rock pools: Palm, Whale, Bilgola, Newport, Mona Vale, Collaroy, Dee Why, Curl Curl, Freshwater, Queenscliff, Bondi, Bronte, Coogee and Cronulla. Great for kids, they're regularly drained and scoured clean of oysters, sand and seaweed, and except for Bondi Icebergs they're free (go figure).

Waratah Park Earth Sanctuary (1, E1) This place was once the backdrop for the iconic '60s Australian TV show *Skippy the Bush Kangaroo*. The new owners demolished the grim old cages and constructed this rambling free-range wildlife park. Count mammals as kangaroos, bandicoots, potoroos and wallabies come out to sniff the sunset BBQ.

☎ 9986 1788 🖳 www .esl.com.au ✉ 13 Namba Rd, Duffys Forest 💲 16.50/11.50 🕑 4-9pm 🚍 30min from Sydney ♿ good 🅿 free

QUIRKY SYDNEY

Barber Records (6, B3) Michael the barber will give you a $20 short back 'n' sides while you listen to records from his sizable jazz, swing, blues and classic rock collection. He also sells weird books, cult videos and other unexpectedly interesting stuff — maybe a 'How to Play Banjo' guide is what you've been yearning for.

☎ 9331 8832 ✉ 275 Victoria St, Darlinghurst 🕑 9am-6pm Mon-Sat 🚉 Kings Cross 🚍 330, 323-7, 365, 366, 387, L24

Camperdown Cemetery (2, B5) Take a self-guided tour beyond the monstrous 1848 fig tree into this dark, eerily unkempt cemetery. Many famous early Australians were buried here between 1849 and 1942, including Eliza Donnithorne, the inspiration for Miss Havisham in Dickens' *Great Expectations*.

☎ 9557 2043 ✉ 187 Church St, Newtown 💲 free, tour brochures near the fig tree 🕑 6am-7pm 🚉 Newtown 🚍 355, 370, 422-3, 426, 428 ♿ good

Destiny Tours (6, C2) Under the cover of darkness, climb into 'Elvira' — a black 1967 Cadillac hearse — and embark on a sexy, sleazy, fun and factual tour of Sydney's seamy underbelly. Sordid tales of convicts, crime, celebrities, scandals and ghosts unfurl as you rattle the skeletons in Sydney's closet.

☎ 0414 232 244 🖳 www.destinytours .com.au ✉ tours depart cnr Ward Ave & Elizabeth Bay Rd, Kings Cross 💲 69 🕑 8-10.30pm 🚉 Kings Cross

Friend in Hand (2, B4) This place has changed the rules of what's supposed to happen in an Australian pub. Sure, you can drink all the beer you want, but don't be surprised when the eating competitions, water-pistol fights, crab racing, stand-up comedians, cheesy Joel/John piano men and hula-hoop spin-offs cut into your drinking time.

☎ 9660 2326 🖳 www .friendinhand.com.au ✉ 58 Cowper Rd, Glebe 💲 free 🕑 10am-5pm

Mon-Sat, noon-10pm Sun 🚌 431-4 ♿ fair

Goat Island (2, C3) A summary: In colonial days, water police hunted smugglers and escaped convicts from this atoll. It's also been a prison, shipyard, quarantine station and gunpowder depot. More recently, the TV cop show *Water Rats* was filmed here. Goat Island 'Heritage Tours' will tell you the rest.
☎ 9247 5033 💻 www .npws.nsw.gov.au ✉ tours depart Cadmans Cottage, 110 George St, The Rocks 💲 19.80/15.40/61.60 🕒 12.30pm Wed & Sat, 1pm Sun 🚆 🚌 🚢 Circular Quay ♿ fair

Eternity

From 1930 to 1967, the word 'Eternity' – beautifully scripted in yellow chalk – appeared almost half a million times on the pavements of inner Sydney. It was written by Arthur Stace, an almost illiterate, hard-drinking petty criminal who, after attending a fire-and-brimstone sermon at a Baptist church in 1930, dropped the bottle and picked up the chalk. Stace's word lit up the Harbour Bridge on New Year's Eve 2000 and a metal replica of his 'Eternity' can be seen at Town Hall Square (5, D7).

Speakers' Corner (5, F5) Recline on a patch of lawn in front of the Art Gallery of NSW and listen to religious zealots, nutters, political extremists, homophobes, hippies and academics express their earnest opinions. Some of them have something interesting to say; some of them are just plain mad. Either way, it makes for an interesting afternoon. BYO soapbox.
✉ Art Gallery Rd, The Domain 💲 free 🕒 noon-4pm Sun 🚆 St James ♿ excellent

SYDNEY FOR CHILDREN

Many places put on activities for children during the school holidays (December/January; April, July and September). Check out www.sydney forkids.com.au for lists of activities geared towards ankle-biters, or the free monthly magazine *Sydney's Child*. The 🚼 icon elsewhere in this book indicates child-friendly venues.

Art Gallery of NSW (5, F6) The Sunday Funday activity programme at the Art Gallery of NSW includes dance, stories, magic, cartoons, Aboriginal performance and exhibition-specific events. Tours of the Asian Gallery with Zhenmu Shou, the ghostly guide from the grave, are a complete blast from the past.
☎ 9225 1744 💻 www .artgallery.nsw.gov .au ✉ Art Gallery Rd, The Domain 💲 free 🕒 2.30pm Sun ♿ good 🚆 St James 🚌 200

Australian Theatre for Young People (5, C2) If your kids dream about running away to the circus, they can start their juggling and sword-swallowing training here. The ATYP runs programmes for eight-year-olds and over, and fills their week with lots of clowning around.
☎ 9251 3900 💻 www .atyp.com.au ✉ Pier 4, 5 Hickson Rd, Walsh Bay 💲 210-465/wk 🕒 holiday programme 10am-6pm Mon-Fri 🚆 🚢 Circular Quay 🚌 430-4, shuttle from Queen Victoria Bldg

Lollipops at Fox Studios (2, D5) Inside the colossal Fox Studios complex Lollipops is a multistorey, exploratory funhouse with ball pits, mazes, tunnels and nets. There's also two free, outdoor, state-of-the-art playgrounds built on bouncy matting for spills 'n' thrills.
☎ 9331 0811 💻 www .lollipopsplayland.com.au ✉ Shop 201 Bent St, Fox Studios (Lang Rd, Moore Park) 💲 4/7.90-10.90 🕒 9.30am-7pm Mon-Fri, 9am-7pm Sat & Sun 🚌 339, 372, 377, 390-9 ♿ good

Kids' Zone, Royal Botanic Gardens (5, E5) The RBG runs a dynamic educational programme of school and community talks and tours for kids, revolving steadily around a theme of dirt and things that grow in it. Recent highlights have included the 'Get Green Thumbs' and 'Poo, Worms & Maggots' sessions.
☎ 9231 8111 ▯ www .rbgsyd.nsw.gov.au/edu cation_kids_zone ✉ Mrs Macquaries Rd $ free ⚇ Circular Quay, Martin Place ⛟ ⚓ Circular Quay

Leuralla Toy & Railway Museum (1, A2) Inside an Art Deco mansion set in misty mountain conifer gardens, this amazing collection of toys from the last two centuries includes china dolls, ships, planes, soldiers and stalwarts like Noddy, Rupert Bear and Barbie. The Railway Museum features a decent-sized Matterhorn and a whole mess of NSW railway memorabilia.
☎ 4784 1169 ▯ www .toyandrailwaymuseum .com.au ✉ 36 Olympian Pde, Leura, Blue Mountains $ 10/5, garden only 6/3 ⌚ 10am-5pm ⚇ CityRail from Central (hourly) 🚗 2hr from Sydney ♿ garden only

Luna Park (2, C3) Luna Park (1935), with its vaguely sinister chip-toothed clown entry, has been periodically closed by noise police in recent decades. It's due to re-open (quietly) in late 2004 — call for opening hours and admission. The rollercoaster may be a bit

Indestructible playground, Fox Studios

less rattly, but the kids will still love it.
☎ 9922 6644 ▯ www .lunaparksydney.com ✉ 1 Olympic Pl, Milsons Point ⚇ Milsons Point ⚓ Kirribilli

Manly Quarantine Station (2, F2) Calling all junior Ghostbusters... this former Quarantine Station is undoubtedly haunted and its two-hour lantern-led ghost tours are designed to inform and entertain by tapping into kids' love of the spooky. Bookings and prepayment essential.
☎ 9347 5033 ▯ www .npws.nsw.gov.au ✉ North Head Scenic Dr, Manly $ 13.20 ⌚ 6-8pm Fri (7-9pm summer) ⛟ 135 (irregular, ☎ 131 500 for details)

Oceanworld (4, A2) See p28.

Sydney Aquarium (5, C6) See p28.

Taronga Zoo (2, D3) See p24.

Toy Museum & Puppet Cottage (5, D3) Hundreds of rare toys, trains, wacky wind-ups, robots and dolls shoulder up to each other in this wondrous two-storey toy museum. The free weekend puppet shows put Punch & Judy to shame.
☎ 9251 8804 ✉ 2-6 Kendall La, The Rocks $ free ⌚ 10am-5.30pm; puppet shows 11am, 12.30pm & 2pm Sat & Sun ⚇ ⛟ ⚓ Circular Quay ♿ ground floor only

Babysitters

The **Wright Nanny** (☎ 9929 7341) supplies first-aid-qualified babysitters and nannies to the whole Sydney area. A casual nanny costs $16/hr, while babysitters are $15/hr. An $18 agency fee applies to all nannies, babysitters and Mary Poppinses. **Lollipops at Fox Studios** also has child care facilities (p36).

Out & About

WALKING TOURS
Hyde Park to the Harbour

This walk makes a stellar introduction to Sydney. Start at the southern end of city oasis **Hyde Park** (**1**), stroll past the **Anzac Memorial** (**2**; p26), stop in for a peek at the **Australian Museum** (**3**; p26) on College St, then re-enter Hyde Park to check out the ludicrously ornate **Archibald Fountain** (**4**). Head east to the venerable **St Mary's Cathedral** (**5**; p27), then curl around Prince Albert Rd to Macquarie St where a procession of refined public buildings awaits.

distance 3km
duration 2hr
▶ **start** 🚇 Museum
● **end** 🚇 🚌 ⛴ Circular Quay

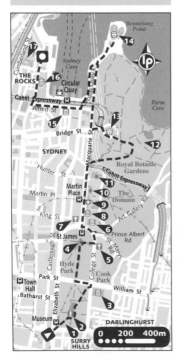

Introducing Sydney: Archibald to Opera

First there's **Hyde Park Barracks Museum** (**6**; p26) which has a cool café if you're hungry, then opposite, **St James Church** (**7**; p27). Continue past twin buildings the **Mint** (**8**; p26) and **Sydney Hospital** (**9**; p26) – polish the Little Boar statue's snout for good luck. **Parliament House** (**10**; p27) and the **State Library of NSW** (**11**) are next, then cut through the **Royal Botanic Gardens** (**12**; p17), up past the **Conservatorium of Music** (**13**; p90) and continue north along Macquarie St to the universally cherished **Sydney Opera House** (**14**; p12).

Re-caffeinate at a Circular Quay East café, then suss out the **Customs House** (**15**; p26) on Alfred St and the **Museum of Contemporary Art** (**16**; p27). Gorge yourself on history in **The Rocks** (**17**; p14), then shake it back to Circular Quay for a ride somewhere else.

Bondi to Bronte Clifftop Trail

This windswept walk heads south from Bondi Beach along the clifftops to Bronte Beach, interweaving panoramic views, swimming spots and beachside foody delights.

Begin at the **Aboriginal rock engravings** (**1**) at Bondi Beach Golf Club (p116; between the tower and the cliffs). March south along Military Rd, turn left into Ramsgate Ave then taste the sea-spray on your face at the **lookout** (**2**). From here the trail runs along the rocks to the beach – if the surf's humongous, stick to Ramsgate Ave and stay dry. Have a quick dip then rummage through Sunday's **Bondi Beach Market** (**3**; p49) for funky miscellanea or stick your head into **Bondi Pavilion** (**4**; p9) for an exhibition or performance.

Grab a bite, a bikini or some surfboard wax on **Campbell Parade** (**5**) then promenade along the beach to Notts Ave and the glistening **Bondi Icebergs** (**6**; p64) pool and restaurant. Step onto the cliff path at the end of Notts Ave – the blustery sandstone cliffs and grinding Pacific Ocean couldn't be more spectacular (look out for dolphins, whales and surfers). Mid-November's **Sculpture by the Sea** (p80) installations along these cliffs

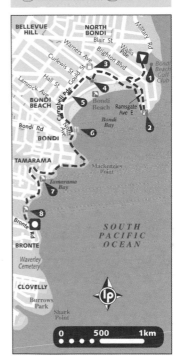

distance 4km
duration 2hr 45min
▶ **start** North Bondi 🚌 380, 389 or L82 from Circular Quay, 381-2 from Bondi Junction
● **end** Bronte Beach 🚌 378

are dramatic and engaging. Slide past sex-pot **Tamarama Beach** (**7**; p33) to **Bronte Beach** (**8**; p32) where beachy cafés will resuscitate you.

Sun, sand and surf: North Bondi panorama

Paddington Perspectives

Ain't no denying it, Paddington is pretty. Hit the back streets for an insider's perspective on how upper-crust Sydney splashes its cash.

Start at the **Victoria Barracks** (**1**; p28) – tour the regal Empirical architecture on Thursdays. Trudge west down Oxford St to Glenmore Rd where a hub of **galleries** (**2**; p29) convenes around Mary Pl. Backtrack to Gipps St; **Paddington's oldest terraces** (**3**) are at the Prospect St corner, built in the 1840s

Paddington Terraces – show me the money

for the barracks' stonemasons. Turn left onto Liverpool St then right at Walker La for **Hogarth Galleries** (**4**; p31). Continue down Liverpool St past moneyed terraces then right onto Glenmore Rd. Three hundred metres past more affluent terraces, Beamers and Mercs is **Five Ways** (**5**), Paddo's old civic centre. Quaff a pint at the **Royal Hotel** (**6**; p77) or a coffee at **Gusto** (**7**; p77).

Continue down Glenmore Rd then veer right into Gurner St; **Wagner Art Gallery** (**8**; p30) is on the Norfolk St corner. Turn right at Cascade St and mooch uphill past more terraces blessed with the photogene. Hang right into Paddington St then left for the glam **William St boutiques** (**9**; p51). Back on Oxford St, bee line for Saturday's **Paddington Bazaar** (**10**; p49) or **Centennial Park** (**11**; p22).

Bags of shopportunities on Oxford St

distance 2.5km
duration 2hr
▶ **start** 🚌 325, 378, 380, L82
● **end** 🚌 325, 378, 380, L82

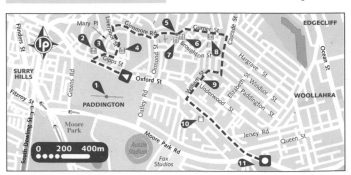

Manly Scenic Walkway

This walk tracks west from Manly around North and Middle Harbour past waterside mansions, harbour viewpoints and through the pristinely rugged Sydney Harbour National Park (wear strong shoes).

> **Duke of Hazard**
> Damn lucky Prince Alfred, Duke of Edinburgh, survived an assassination attempt on Clontarf Beach in 1868. The bullet gave him a good whang, but his rubber braces absorbed most of the impact.

Check the surf at **Manly Beach** (**1**; p23) then buy yourself a picnic lunch on The Corso before heading to **Oceanworld** (**2**; p28) on West Esplanade. Scan the view through the Heads from **Fairlight** (**3**) and the yachts tugging on their moorings near **Forty Baskets Beach** (**4**). Listen for kookaburras as you enter the **Sydney Harbour National Park** (**5**; p10) and approach **Reef Beach** (**6**). The track becomes steep, sandy and rocky further into the park – look for wildflowers, fat goannas sunning themselves and spiders in bottlebrush trees. The views from **Dobroyd Head** (**7**) are unforgettable. Check out the **deserted 1930s sea shanties** (**8**) at the base of Crater Cove cliff and **Aboriginal rock carvings** (**9**) on an unsigned ledge left of the track before the **Grotto Point Lighthouse** (**10**) turn-off. Quiet, calm **Castle Rock Beach** (**11**) at the western end of the national park is a super spot for lunch, or hit the picnic tables at Tania Park and **Clontarf Beach** (**12**). Bus it back to the city from the southern end of **The Spit Bridge** (**13**).

distance 10km
duration 4hr
▶ **start** 🚶 Manly 🚌 151,169, E69 from Wynyard Park
● **end** 🚌 151,169, E69 from Wynyard Park

Strong shoes? Rugged Sydney Harbour NP

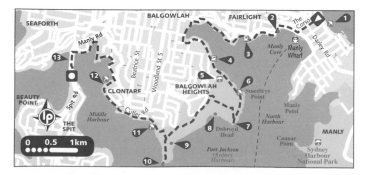

DAY TRIPS
National Parks
KU-RING-GAI CHASE
NATIONAL PARK   (1, E1)

This 15,000-hectare park has that classic Sydney cocktail of bushland, sandstone outcrops and water vistas, plus walking tracks, horse-riding trails, picnic areas and Aboriginal rock engravings. Make a full day of it.

Elevated parts of the park offer **glorious water views** over Cowan Creek, Broken Bay and Pittwater. The view from West Head across Pittwater to Barrenjoey Head is also fantastic. Elusive **lyrebirds** are conspicuous at West Head during their May-to-July mating period. There are **Aboriginal engravings** on the Basin Track and Garigal Aboriginal Heritage Walk, and a mangrove boardwalk from the Bobbin Head carpark.

Halvorsen Boats (☎ 9457 9011) rents row and motorboats from Bobbin Head. Sharks in Broken Bay make for a risky swim, but there's a netted area at The Basin if you simply *must* cool off.

INFORMATION
24km north of Sydney
- 🚗 45min from Sydney
- 🚆 Turramurra then 🚌 577 to Bobbin Head Gate
- 💻 www.nationalparks.nsw.gov.au
- 💲 11/car
- 🕑 sunrise-sunset
- ℹ Bobbin Head Information Centre (☎ 9472 8949; Bobbin Head Rd; 🕑 10am-4pm) & Kalkari Visitors Centre (☎ 9472 9300; Ku-ring-gai Chase Rd; 🕑 9am-5pm). Kalkari runs guided tours.
- 🍴 café at Bobbin Head, Akuna Bay Restaurant (☎ 9450 2660)

Lyrebird, where? Ku-ring-gai Chase NP

ROYAL NATIONAL PARK   (1, D3)

The traditional lands of the Dharawal people, Royal National Park, established in 1879, is the oldest National Park in the world. It features vertiginous cliffs, secluded beaches, coastal scrub, lush rainforest and isolated seaside communities.

INFORMATION
30km south of Sydney
- 🚗 45min from Sydney
- 🚆 Cronulla then 🚢 to Bundeena
- 💻 www.nationalparks.nsw.gov.au
- 💲 11/car
- 🕑 main roads 24hr, beach roads close at sunset
- ℹ Visitors Centre (☎ 9542 0648; Audley entrance; 🕑 9.30am-4.30pm)
- 🍴 Bundeena

The main road through the park detours to **Bundeena**, a small town on Port Hacking – a world away from Sydney's clash and throb. There are a couple of fish-and-chip shops and beachy B&Bs if you want to stay the night. Further into the park is **Wattamolla Beach**, empty and great for a swim, and **Garie Beach**, empty and great for a surf.

Audley Boatshed (☎ 9528 9867) rents rowboats, kayaks, canoes and bikes. There are some super picnic sites, walks and cycling tracks in the park – contact the visitors centre for information.

Northern Beaches (1, E1-2)

Sydney's Northern Beaches are sublime. Tracking north from Manly, they form a continuous 30km stretch of laid-back suburbs, craggy headlands, orange beaches, solid surf and fish-and-chip shops by the dozen – a great place to spend a day exploring, swimming, surfing, eating or chilling out as the beach-break pummels the shore.

From north to south, here's the low-down: **Palm Beach** is a long orange arc capped by **Barrenjoey Lighthouse** (tours ☎ 9451 3479). Nudists nude-up to the north; million-dollar real estate booms in the south. Cheeseball TV soap *Home & Away* is filmed somewhere in between. With Norfolk Island pines and steep cliffs, **Whale Beach** is underrated – a paradise slice with real estate set to rocket. **Avalon** is

INFORMATION
30km north of Sydney
🚌 45min from Sydney
🚢 Manly
🚌 151,169, E69 city to Manly; L90 & 190 city to Palm Beach
🖥 www.sydneynorthernbeaches.com.au
ℹ Manly Visitors Centre (☎ 9977 1088; Manly Wharf; ☻ 9am-5pm Mon-Fri, 10am-4pm Sat & Sun)
🍴 see p78

a sleepy hollow with cool cafés and serious surf. When the producers of *Baywatch* wanted to film here in the '90s, locals told them to bugger off. Down 'The Serpentine', **Bilgola** feels like a well kept local secret. Erring on the side of suburbia, **Newport** is saved by its wide beach and rocky breaks. For great coastal views, trek up Hillcrest Ave to the lookout between **Bungan** and **Mona Vale** beaches. **Warriewood** is unpretentious and uncrowded. Elongated **Narrabeen** chases the endless summer south to **Collaroy** – high-rise apartments, high-rise surf. Families and *Big Wednesday* breaks prevail at **Dee Why**. **Curl Curl** is the most democratic of the Northern Beaches with middle-sized waves and incomes. **Freshwater** is so small it'd be overlooked if it weren't for all the apartments overlooking it. **Manly** (p23) is King of the Northern Beaches.

Nude-up at Palm Beach north, or peruse the views from Barrenjoey Lighthouse

The Blue Mountains (1, B1-2)

The Blue Mountains, part of the Great Dividing Range, offer jaw-dropping scenery, bushwalks, gorges, gums and gourmet restaurants galore. Relaxed mountain towns **Katoomba**, **Leura** and **Wentworth Falls** (see p25) are well worth exploring.

Three Sisters: rock-solid sorority

Katoomba's many Art Deco cafés, descending mists and occasional snowfalls are otherworldly. Two kilometres down Katoomba St from the Carrington Hotel (the town's historic heart) tour buses gather at **Echo Point**. Significant to local Aborigines, the **Three Sisters** rock formation stands sentinel as clouds drift through the **Jamison Valley** treetops below.

West of here is **Scenic World** (☎ 4782 2699; www.scenicworld.com.au; cnr Cliff Dve & Violet St,

Purple Haze

The bluish haze which gives the Blue Mountains their name comes from the fine mist of eucalyptus oil exuded by gum trees.

Katoomba; $14/7 return; ♿ good). If you can stomach the multistorey megaplex vibe and blaring theme from *Raiders of the Lost Ark*, ride the 1880s railway down the 52° incline to the valley floor. Wander the 2km forest boardwalk or the 12km-return track to the **Ruined Castle** rock formation then catch the Sceniscender cable car back up the slope.

The **Purse Museum** (☎ 4782 7588; www.pursemuseum.com.au, 277 Katoomba St, Katoomba) has an astonishing collection of 500 purses from 1650 to the present day.

The **Norman Lindsay Gallery & Museum** (☎ 4751 1067; www.hermes.net.au/nlg; 14 Norman Lindsay Cres, Faulconbridge; $9/6; ☷ 10am-4pm), former home of the Australian author, artist and *bon vivant*, contains many of his paintings, cartoons, illustrations and sculptures.

The National Parks and Wildlife Service (NPWS) and several companies offer tours and adventure activities; consult Echo Point visitors centre. Locals open their gardens to visitors during spring and autumn **garden festivals**. The **Blue Mountains Music Festival** happens in March. Check out **Leuralla Toy & Railway Museum** (p37) in Leura and the **Jenolan Caves** 1¼hr west of Katoomba.

Parramatta (1, D2)

Parramatta, derived from a Daruag Aboriginal name meaning 'the place where eels lie down', was Australia's second European settlement. Sydney's sandy soils were lousy for growing carrots, so Parramatta's river plains were chosen instead.

The town has been subsumed by Sydney's endless western suburbs and has weathered some hideous architectural disservices, but retains a small-town vibe and a clutch of precious colonial buildings. Ride the **RiverCat** (☎ 131 500; www.131500.com.au; $14/7 return) from Circular Quay – Sydney Harbour thins into the lazy, waterlily-laden Parramatta River, just 25m across.

The **Old Government House** (☎ 9635 8149; Parramatta Park; $8/5/18; ☾ 1hr tours 10am-4.30pm Mon-Fri, 10.30am-4 30pm Sat-Sun; ☧ ground floor only), established in 1799, was Parramatta's first farm and housed successive NSW governors until the 1850s.

> **INFORMATION**
> *24km west of Sydney*
> 🚢 RiverCat from Circular Quay
> 🚆 Parramatta
> 🚌 L20, 520 from Circular Quay
> 🚗 45min from Sydney
> 💻 www.parracity.nsw.gov.au
> ℹ️ Parramatta Heritage Centre
>   (☎ 8839 3322; 346a Church St;
>   ☾ 9am-5pm)
> 🍴 Ziggy's (☎ 9687 1588; 285 Church St), Harris Farm Market Café (☎ 9895 1900; Riverbank Centre, 330 Church St)

Elizabeth Farm (☎ 9635 9488; www.hht.nsw.gov.au; 70 Alice St; $7/3/17; ☾ 10am-5pm; ☧ excellent), Australia's oldest surviving European home (1793), was built by renegade pastoralist/rum trader John Macarthur and his wife Elizabeth. It's now an innovative hands-on museum – recline on the furniture and thumb through Elizabeth's letters.

Hambledon Cottage (☎ 9635 6924; cnr Hassall St & Gregory Pl; $4/3; ☾ 11am-4pm Wed, Thu, Sat & Sun; ☧ good), built in 1824 for the Macarthurs' daughter's governess, was later used as Elizabeth Farm's weekend lodgings and almost became a carpark in the '80s.

Governor Phillip built **Experiment Farm Cottage** (☎ 9635 5655; 9 Ruse St; $5.50/4/14; ☾ 10.30am-3.30pm Tue-Fri, 11am-3.30pm Sat & Sun) in 1791 for emancipist farmer James Ruse as an experiment to see how long it would take him to wean himself from government supplies.

The **Parramatta Eels** (☎ 9683 6311; www.parraeels.com.au; O'Connell St), glam Rugby League team of the '80s, collide at Parramatta Stadium.

Prospective Parramatta Eels hard at play

ORGANISED TOURS

Bush & Adventure Tours

High 'n' Wild (1, A2)
Feeling like busting out of the city for some extreme outdoor action? These guys run full- and half-day abseiling, canyoning, rock climbing, bushwalking, mountain biking and mountaineering adventures from Katoomba. ☎ 4782 6224 🖥 www.high-n-wild.com.au ✉ 3-5 Katoomba St, Katoomba 💲 79-99/125-149 half/full day 🕑 tours depart 9am

Oz Trails Hyper-friendly tour guides wheel you around the Blue Mountains to the Nepean River, Kings Tableland, Evans Lookout, Wentworth Falls, Leura, Katoomba, Echo Point, Scenic World and Olympic Park, finishing with a ride back to Circular Quay on the Parramatta River. ☎ 9387 8380, 0411 288 805 🖥 www.oztrails.com.au ✉ hotel pickup 💲 83 full-day tour 🕑 8am-6pm

Harbour Cruises

Captain Cook Cruises (5, D4) CCC run hop-on, hop-off Sydney Harbour Explorer cruises. Dodging windsurfers, ferries, 18ft skiffs and a full menagerie of other harbour craft, they scoot around between The Rocks, Watsons Bay, Taronga Zoo & Darling Harbour. ☎ 9206 1111 🖥 www.captaincook.com.au ✉ Wharf 6, Circular Quay 💲 25/12/55 2hr cruise 🕑 8.30am-7.30pm

EastSail (6, E2) Eastsail lets you swing the boom and hoist the mainsail on morning yacht cruises, or make a decadent night of it with an 'Overnight Indulgence' – a two-hour twilight sail followed by dinner and breakfast at a secure mooring. What you do in between meals is up to you... ☎ 9327 1166 🖥 www.eastsail.com.au ✉ d'Albora Marina, New Beach Rd, Rushcutters Bay 💲 89 morning cruise, $699 overnight 🕑 10am morning cruise, 5.30pm overnight

Harbour Island Tours
See p10.

James Craig (5, B5) The *James Craig* is a hulking three-masted black-hulled iron barque built in Sunderland, England in 1874. Abandoned in Tasmania in the '30s, she was floated to Sydney and restored in the '70s. Square-rigged sails billow as you sail out through the Heads on the open-ocean swell. Price includes lunch, morning/afternoon teas and a sea shanty or three. ☎ 9298 3888 🖥 www.austfleet.com ✉ Wharf 7, Pyrmont 💲 187 🕑 9.30am-4pm every 2nd weekend

Matilda Cruises (5, C6) Matilda's proud armada of catamarans, yachts and ferries will float you out onto the water and zoom you 'round all of Sydney's main harbour sights on a one-hour Rocket Tour. Full-day sailing adventures and luxurious cocktail dinner cruises are also available. ☎ 9264 7377 🖥 www.matilda.com.au ✉ Pier 6, Aquarium Wharf, Darling Harbour & Wharf 6 Circular Quay 💲 22/17.60/49.50 🕑 9am-8pm

Sydney Ferries (5, D4) If anyone's got the credentials to show you Sydney Harbour, it's Sydney Ferries. One-hour to 2½-hour morning, afternoon and evening harbour sights and lights cruises are available, chugging around on Sydney's cherished old ferries. ☎ 9207 3170 🖥 www.sydneyferries.nsw.gov.au ✉ Wharf 4, Circular Quay 💲 15-22/7.50-11/37/47.50 🕑 morning 8am;

BridgeClimb – high, wide and handsome

afternoon 1pm Mon-Fri, 12.30pm Sat & Sun; evening 8pm Mon-Sat

Other Tours

BridgeClimb (5, D3) Once only painters and daredevils scaled the Harbour Bridge heights – now anyone can do it. Once you're through the departure lounge and extensive training session, don your headset, umbilical cord and dandy grey jumpsuit (Elvis would be so proud) and up you go.
☎ 8274 7777 💻 www .bridgeclimb.com ✉ 5 Cumberland St, The Rocks 💲 155/175 normal/peak 🕑 3½hr tours around the clock

Destiny Tours
See p35.

Night Cat Tours Experience the good, the bad and the ugly of nocturnal Sydney with a Night Cat tour through the city, Balmain, Newtown, Paddington, Bondi, Woolloomooloo and Kings Cross. Small groups get the inside running on Sydney's history, facts and fiction – a salubrious 'Tiger' pie for dinner at **Harry's Cafe de Wheels** (p73) is a showstopper.
☎ 1300 551 608 💻 www.nightcattours .com ✉ tour departs Central Station, Kings Cross & Circular Quay 💲 65/55 🕑 6.30-11.30pm

Sydney by Seaplane (2, E4) Whether it's a 15-minute harbour flyby or a longer jaunt over Palm Beach, Parramatta and the Hawkesbury River, Sydney by Seaplane

Arachnophobia

The Sydney funnel-web spider (*Atrax robustus*) is nasty piece of work. Nomadic, aggressive and hugely poisonous with fangs that can pierce a toenail, they're formidable beasts. They generally malinger in bushland under leaf litter and dead wood, but often go wandering around after rains (no, not in the city). They've caused a handful of deaths in modern history, but none since the development of an antivenin in 1981. You'd be extremely unlucky to cop a fang-full, but if you do, stay cool and get to a hospital within a couple of hours and you'll be fine.

will knock your socks off. Can't get a booking? Try **Sydney Harbour Seaplanes** (☎ 1300 732 752) at the same venue.
☎ 1300 656 787 💻 www.sydneybysea plane.com ✉ Rose Bay Seaplane Base, Lyne Park, Rose Bay 💲 145/220/330 🕑 15, 30 & 50min flights via booking

Scenic Wine Tasting Tour Wax lyrical about toasty noses, full-berry aromas and tart finishes on this full-day minibus booze-cruise of the Hunter Valley, home to over 70 wineries 180km north of Sydney. Tours include wine tastings at three vineyards, commentary, coffee with kangaroos, lunch, a chocolate adventure and a cheese-to-wine matching session – savour the flavour!
☎ 9967 3238 💻 www .redcarpettours.com .au ✉ hotel pick-up 💲 135/125 🕑 8am-6pm

Cultural Tours

Rocks Walking Tours (5, D3)
See p14.

Sydney Aboriginal Discoveries This outfit runs several different tours focusing on Aboriginal culture and history, including walkabout tours of Sydney's indigenous landmarks and sacred sites, a tasty feast of native Australian foods and a Dreamtime cruise. Call for info on departure points, times and tour options.
☎ 8850 3291, 0405 289 016 💻 www.sydneyaus tour.com.au/Abordiscover .html ✉ departure points vary 💲 65-180 🕑 2-4hr tours daily

Sydney Architecture Walks (5, D4) Woah, who designed *that* gorgeous hacienda/heinous behemoth? These bright young archi-buffs run four themed walking tours: Sydney Opera House, Public Art, Harbour Features & Buildings and Urban Patterns of Sydney. Call for bookings and departure times.
☎ 9518 6866 💻 www .sydneyarchitecture.org ✉ tours depart Museum of Sydney, cnr Bridge & Phillip Sts 💲 20/15 🕑 2hr walks, rain or shine

Shopping

Sydney's brash, ingrained culture of commercialism goes a long way towards explaining its citizens' passion for shopping. Most locals treat it as recreational activity rather than a necessity, evidenced by the teeming, cash-flapping masses at the city's numerous weekend markets.

Shopping in central Sydney can be fun, but hectic. The **CBD** is brimming over with department, chain and international fashion stores – shopping here is about as fast and furious as Australia gets. Much more chilled-out are inner-city shopping strips in suburbs like **Paddington**, **Glebe** and **Newtown** – long, sinuous swathes of boutiques, cafés and bookshops.

You can buy everything from gumboots to G-strings in Sydney's shops, but some of the more interesting stuff is in the galleries – **Aboriginal art** (p31) and cutting-edge craft (glass and jewellery) in particular.

How Would You Like To Pay For That?

All stores accept major credit cards but identification – a valid driving licence or passport – is required when using travellers cheques. A 10% Federal Goods and Services Tax (GST) is automatically included in the price of most things you buy. Visitors to Australia are entitled to a refund of any GST paid on items over $300 from one supplier. See p111 for details.

Bargaining and haggling isn't really part of Australian consumer culture – locals tend to think it's somehow undignified and shop around for the best prices instead – but it may work for you at duty-free stores and markets. Most larger stores will arrange shipment or mailing of bulky or fragile items.

Top Spots to Shop

Sydney's main shopping areas are:

City Centre – major department and chain stores, boutiques, duty-free shops, Australiana and outdoor gear.

The Rocks – opal stores, Australiana and Aboriginal art.

Oxford St, Paddington & Darlinghurst – hip boutiques, bookshops, homewares and speciality stores.

Queen St, Woollahra – antiques and art galleries.

Double Bay – designer boutiques, expensive children's wear.

King St, Newtown & Crown St, Darlinghurst – quirky clothing, record shops, furniture and giftware.

Balmain & Glebe – bookshops, vintage clothing, one-off boutiques.

Smilin' and stylin': Sydney always looks good

Opening Hours

Most stores are open from 9.30am to 6pm Monday to Wednesday and Friday and until 5pm on Saturday, with late-night shopping until 9pm on Thursdays. Sunday trading is increasingly popular, but expect shorter hours: typically 11am to 5pm. Sales are usually held in early January and July.

MARKETS

Balmain Market (2, B4)
Milling around the shady grounds of St Andrews Congregational, stalls selling arts, crafts, books, clothing, jewellery, plants and fruit and veg jumble together like socks in a drawer. There's a pavement art exhibition, and the church itself is open if you want a Middle Eastern snack or need to consult St Andy about a prospective purchase.
☎ 0418 765 736 ✉ cnr Darling St & Curtis Rd ⏱ 8.30am-4pm Sat 🚌 431-4, 441-2, 445-6

Bondi Beach Market
(3, B1) Remember the days of the old school yard? We used to laugh a lot... The kids are at the beach on Sundays while their school fills up with Bondi groovers rummaging through funky second-hand clothes and books, hippy beads and earrings, aromatherapy oils, candles, old Cat Stevens records...
☎ 9315 8988 ✉ Bondi Beach Public School, cnr Campbell Pde & Warners Ave ⏱ 9am-4pm Sun 🚌 380, 389 or L82 from Circular Quay, 381-2 from Bondi Junction

Fox Studio's Farmers Market (2, D5)
See p56.

Glebe Market (2, B5)
If you missed Woodstock, you'll find its dreadlocked, shoeless legacy here. Inner-city hippies and ferals beat a hazy course to this crowded market every Saturday.

Once massaged, fuelled on lentil burgers and swathed in funky retro gear, they kick back on the lawns, pass the peace pipe and chill out to a soundtrack of bongos and wind chimes.
☎ 4237 7499 ✉ Glebe Public School, cnr Glebe Point Rd & Derby Pl ⏱ 9am-4pm Sat 🚌 431-4

Good Living Growers Market (5, A6)
See p56.

Paddington Bazaar (6, D5)
Sydney's most-attended weekend market in and around the Paddington Uniting Church coughs up everything from vintage clothes and hip-designer fashions to jewellery, kooky books, foot massage and palmistry. Parking is a misery – take public transport. When the buskers, babies and boisterous crowd wear thin, repair to a Paddo pub for lunch (p77).
☎ 9331 2923 ✉ 395 Oxford St ⏱ 10am-4pm Sat, to 5pm summer 🚌 325, 378, 380, L82

Paddy's Market (5, C9)
Paddy's is the Sydney equivalent of Istanbul's Grand Bazaar, but swap the incense, hookahs and carpets for mobile phone covers, Wu-Tang T-shirts and cheap running shoes. There's over 1000 stalls in this cavernous space – pick up a VB singlet for Uncle Bruce or wander the aisles in capitalist awe.
☎ 1300 361 589 🖥 www.paddysmarkets

.com.au ✉ cnr Hay & Thomas Sts, Haymarket ⏱ 9am-5pm Thu-Sun 🚉 Central Ⓜ Powerhouse Museum 🚊 Haymarket 🚌 George St buses

The Rocks Market (5, D3)
The promoter's line goes, 'Choose something you like, somewhere you love'. Under a long white canopy the 150 stalls are a little on the touristy Australiana side of the tracks (fossils, opals, faux-Aboriginal art and carved wooden fruit bowls etc) but are still worth a gander. Maybe what you choose to like will be the buskers and a beer at the pub.
☎ 9240 8717 🖥 www.therocksmarket.com ✉ George St, The Rocks (under Sydney Harbour Bridge) ⏱ 10am-5pm Sat & Sun 🚉 🚌 🚢 Circular Quay

Sydney Fish Market (2, B4)
See p57.

Sydney Opera House Market (5, E2)
Under big, cream umbrellas and Opera House arcs, elbow for position in the hunt for high-quality contemporary Australian ceramics, gems, toys, jewellery, hats, paintings, photographs and souvenirs. If the 40 stalls don't satisfy, just dig the architecture.
☎ 9315 8465 ✉ Western Boardwalk, Sydney Opera House, Circular Quay ⏱ 9am-4pm Sun 🚉 🚌 🚢 Circular Quay

DEPARTMENT STORES & SHOPPING CENTRES

Argyle Stores (5, D3) This massive place feels like a 19th-century liquor store and carriage house that's morphed into an open-plan minimall with boutiques, jewellery and homeware shops, art galleries and exhibition spaces interspersing massive eucalypt columns and beams. In fact, that's exactly what it is.
☎ 9251 4800 ✉ 18-24 Argyle St, The Rocks ✇ 10am-6pm Mon-Fri, to 7pm Thu ⓡ ⓡ ⓐ Circular Quay

Broadway Shopping Centre (2, C5) Inside the rejuvenated Grace Bros building (check out the cool old globes), this centre has dozens of shops, food court, cinema complex and two 24-hour supermarkets. There's also a massive Rebel Sports outlet with every conceivable bat, ball, shoe and racket.
☎ 9213 3333 ▢ www .broadway-centre.com.au

✉ cnr Parramatta Rd & Bay St, Glebe ✇ 6am-midnight ⓡ ⓡ Central ⓡ 431-4 Ⓟ multistorey

Chifley Plaza (5, E5) Named after the former Australian prime minister, Chifley Plaza has an austere parliamentary atmosphere. If the towering façade, lofty ceilings and marble floors make you feel insignificant, retail therapy might help: try Max Mara, Crabtree & Evelyn or selected Australians like RM Williams (outback gear) and Bristol & Brook (slick gifts).
☎ 9221 6111 ▢ www .chifleyplaza.com.au ✉ 2 Chifley Sq ✇ 9.30am-6pm Mon-Fri, to 4pm Sat ⓡ Martin Place Ⓟ

David Jones (5, D6) In two enormous city buildings, DJs is considered Sydney's premier department store. The Market St store has menswear, electrical and

a high-brow food court; the Castlereagh St store has women's and children's wear and a friendly concierge to point you in the right direction.
☎ 9266 5737 ▢ www .davidjones.com ✉ cnr Market & Castlereagh Sts ✇ 9.30am-6pm Mon-Fri, to 9pm Thu, 9am-6pm Sat, 11am-5pm Sun ⓡ St James Ⓜ City Centre

Gowings (5, D6) Over five floors, this place is a veritable 'blokeatorium'. Pick up a canoe, a telescope or a hammock on the top floor then filter down past the '$15 – change your life' barber and racks of Hawaiian shirts, boxer shorts and baseball caps. A blue 'Chesty Bonds' singlet is the mandatory man-purchase.
☎ 9287 6394 ▢ www .gowings.com ✉ cnr George & Market Sts ✇ 8.30am-6pm Mon-Fri, to 9pm Thu, 9am-6pm Sat, 10am-5pm Sun ⓡ Town Hall Ⓜ City Centre ⓡ George St buses

Myer (5, D6) Formerly the dowdy Grace Bros, Myer has made a concerted effort to liven things up a bit. Over seven floors, there's everything from hip fashions (Wayne Cooper, Seduce, Chloe) to designer cosmetics (MAC, Chanel), two cafés and a noodle bar.
☎ 9238 9111 ▢ www .colesmyer.com.au ✉ cnr George & Market Sts ✇ 9am-6pm Mon-Sat, to 9pm Thu, 11am-5pm Sun ⓡ Town Hall Ⓜ City

Unchain My Heart

Sydney has a fat smattering of chain stores selling quality clothes, shoes and accessories. Four of the best:

Aquila (6, E5; ☎ 9360 4591; www.aquila.com.au; 460 Oxford St, Paddington) Smart boots for smart suits, plus shoes and sandals for under-heeled blokes.

Country Road (5, D6; ☎ 9394 1823; www.country road.com.au; 142 Pitt St) Stylish, conservative men's and women's clothes for the office or the yacht club.

Industrie (6, D5; ☎ 9361 5333; www.industrie .com.au; 272 Oxford St, Paddington) Up-to-the-nanosecond, affordable street gear for dudes.

Witchery (5, D6; ☎ 9231 1245; www.witchery.com .au; Shop 2G, Sydney Central Plaza, Pitt St Mall) Calvin Klein look-a-like fashion at fractional prices.

Centre 🚌 George St buses ♿ good

Queen Victoria Building (5, D6) The QVB is a high-Victorian masterpiece occupying an entire city block. Yeah, sure, the 200 speciality shops are great, but check out the wrought-iron balconies, stained-glass shopfronts, mosaic floors, tinkling Baby Grand and hyper-kitsch animated Royal Clock (featuring the Battle of Hastings and hourly execution of King Charles I).
☎ 9264 9209 🖥 www .qvb.com.au ✉ 455 George St 🕑 9am-6pm Mon-Sat, to 9pm Thu, 11am-5pm Sun 🚆 Town Hall Ⓜ Galeries Victoria 🚌 George St buses Ⓟ ♿ good

Stranded in The Strand – what a way to go...

Strand Arcade (5, D6) Constructed in 1891 in a squeezy space between George and Pitt Sts, the Strand Arcade rivals the QVB in the ornateness stakes. Three floors of designer fashions, Australiana and old-world coffee shops will make your short cut through here considerably longer.
☎ 9232 4199 🖥 www .strandarcade.com.au ✉ 412 George St & 193-5 Pitt St Mall 🕑 7.30am-6pm Mon-Sat, to 9pm Thu, 11am-4pm Sun 🚆 Town Hall Ⓜ City Centre 🚌 George St buses

CLOTHES & SHOES

Alannah Hill (5, D6) Boudoir belles stock up on beaded handbags, feather boas, fishnet stockings and diaphanous cocktail dresses at this crimson-hued shop. Designs recall an earlier time: one part Louise Brooks with a dash of Josephine Baker and a big sploosh of Lana Turner.
☎ 9221 1251 ✉ L1, Strand Arcade, 412 George St 🕑 9.30am-5.30pm Mon-Fri, to 7pm Thu, to 5pm Sat, 10am-5pm Sun 🚆 Town Hall Ⓜ City Centre 🚌 George St buses

Belinda (6, D5) Belinda stocks a tightly edited collection of Australian designers and expensive international imports. Its second, mildly less wallet-threatening

store **The Corner Shop** (☎ 9380 9828; 43 William St) is a treasure-trove of funky Australian designers. Alternatively, act nonplussed then head for the Bondi Beach Market.
☎ 9380 8728 🖥 www .belinda.com.au ✉ 39 William St 🕑 10am-6pm Mon-Sat, noon-5pm Sun 🚌 378, 380, 382, L82

Calibre (6, D5) Hip, high-calibre Calibre fills the wardrobes of Sydney's power players with schmick suits in seasonal fabrics and colours, plus Gucci sunnies, Costume National shoes, YSL ties and Samsonite briefcases. Gordon Gecko eat your heart out.
☎ 9380 5993 🖥 www

.calibreclothing.com.au ✉ 416 Oxford St, Paddington 🕑 9.30am-6pm Mon-Sat, to 8pm Thu, 10am-6pm Sat, 11.30am-5.30pm Sun 🚌 378, 380, 382, L82

Capital L (6, B4) Owner Louise stocks 52 up-and-coming designers to complement those already in the limelight. Achingly hip sales staff break the Paddo mould and actually help you find and try on clothes by local talents like Cohen & Sabine.
☎ 9361 0111 🖥 www .capital-l.com ✉ 333 South Dowling St, Darlinghurst 🕑 11am-6pm Mon-Fri, to 8pm Thu, 10am-6pm Sat, noon-5pm Sun 🚌 378, 380, 382, L82

Alannah Hill. Our credit card just can't get enough.

Collette Dinnigan (6, D5)
This shop's sanded floors, wrought-iron staircase and courtyard fountain form the perfect backdrop for Collette Dinnigan's beaded dresses and flouncy lingerie. The Hollywood-honed Aussies flock here whenever they need a new frock (Nicole or Naomi might be in the next change room).
☎ 9360 6691 🖳 www .collettedinnigan.com ✉ 33 William St, Paddington ◷ 10am-6pm Mon-Sat, noon-4pm Sun 🚌 378, 380, 382, L82

Dangerfield (5, C9)
Clubbers and teeny boppers get all het up over this shop. There's wall-to-wall low-cut jeans, slogan-proclaiming T-shirts, post-punk studded bracelets, faux-fur handbags and plaid '70s lounge-lizard pants, set to incessantly wailing girl-pop tunes. 'Het up' doesn't begin to describe it.
☎ 9280 3760 ✉ L1, cnr Hay & Thomas Sts,

Haymarket ◷ 10am-7pm, to 8pm Thu 🚇 Town Hall Ⓜ Powerhouse Museum 🚇 Haymarket

DPO (6, D5) DPO zooms in on the dapper street-wear market. Cult denim labels duke it out with custom T-shirts and cool DJ bags. Friendly staff find the time to explain why that pair of $450 jeans is worth every red cent.
☎ 9361 4339; fax 9360 3909 ✉ 439 Oxford St, Paddington ◷ 10am-6pm Mon-Sat, to 8pm Thu, 11am-5pm Sun 🚌 378, 380, 382, L82

Hype DC (5, D6) A true Temple of Trainers, Hype DC scours the planet for the latest shoes by Snipe, Asics, Gola, Lacoste, Puma, Adidas, Vans and Converse (hey, check out those wicked knee-high All-Stars!). All you homies get to steppin'.
☎ 9231 0004 🖳 www .hypedc.com ✉ G, Imperial Arcade, Pitt St Mall

CLOTHING & SHOE SIZES

Women's Clothing

Aust/UK	8	10	12	14	16	18
Europe	36	38	40	42	44	46
Japan	5	7	9	11	13	15
USA	6	8	10	12	14	16

Women's Shoes

Aust/USA	5	6	7	8	9	10
Europe	35	36	37	38	39	40
France only	35	36	38	39	40	42
Japan	22	23	24	25	26	27
UK	3½	4½	5½	6½	7½	8½

Men's Clothing

Aust	92	96	100	104	108	112
Europe	46	48	50	52	54	56

Japan	S	M	M		L	
UK/USA	35	36	37	38	39	40

Men's Shirts (Collar Sizes)

Aust/Japan	38	39	40	41	42	43
Europe	38	39	40	41	42	43
UK/USA	15	15½	16	16½	17	17½

Men's Shoes

Aust/ UK	7	8	9	10	11	12
Europe	41	42	43	44½	46	47
Japan	26	27	27.5	28	29	30
USA	7½	8½	9½	10½	11½	12½

Measurements approximate only; try before you buy.

Divine Designers

Fab, flimsy Australian creations for the size-six disciples of London, Paris and New York's latest statements:

Bettina Liano (5, D6; ☎ 9223 3511; www.bettinaliano.com; L1, Strand Arcade, 412 George St) Famous low-cut butt-hugger jeans.

Bracewell (6, D5; ☎ 9331 5844; www.bracewell.com.au; 274 Oxford St, Paddington) Sexy, structured and sassy; Mavi & Sassbide jeans.

Lisa Ho (6, E6; ☎ 9360 2345; www.lisaho.com.au; 2a Queen St, Woollahra) Sheer party frocks for the social whirlwind that is your life.

Morrissey (6, D5; ☎ 9380 4722; 372 Oxford St, Paddington) Attention high-heeled bubble-chested amber-tan babes – bring your gold credit card.

Wayne Cooper (5, D6; ☎ 9221 5292; www.waynecooper.com.au; L1, Strand Arcade, 412 George St) Release your inner vixen in devilishly brave gear.

Zimmermann (5, D6; ☎ 9221 9558; www.zimmermannwear.com; L1, Strand Arcade, 412 George St) Sydney's best swimwear, hats and suits.

🕙 9am-6.30pm Mon-Sat, to 9pm Thu, 10am-6pm Sun 🚇 St James Ⓜ City Centre

Leona Edmiston (6, D5) Leona Edmiston knows a thing or two about dresses. Her sassy designs have been described as exuberantly feminine, flirtatious and fun, cut from the best seasonal cottons, silks and jerseys in colours that range from luscious, sophisticated reds to pinstripes and polka dots.
☎ 9331 7033 💻 www.leonaedmiston.com.au ✉ 88 William St, Paddington 🕙 10am-6pm Mon-Fri, to 5pm Sat, noon-4pm Sun 🚌 378, 380, 382, L82

Mambo (6, B4) Mambo adheres to a comic creed of beautifully ugly surf design that makes its way onto T-shirts, board shorts, watches, sunglasses, surfboards, backpacks and bikinis. Pumping hip-hop and house shakes the store into a state of frenzied colour and overdriven art.
☎ 9331 8034 💻 www.mambo.com.au ✉ 17 Oxford St, Paddington 🕙 10am-6pm, to 8pm Thu 🚌 378, 380, 382, L82

Marcs (5, D6) Prominent and perfect on the Pitt St Mall, Marcs' delightfully aerated boy-staff will giggle you into directional UK and Euro labels if your pocket can stand the heat. Otherwise, their own hip line of T-shirts, pants and suits won't break the bank.
☎ 9221 5575 💻 www.marcs.com.au ✉ Shop P288, Pitt St Mall 🕙 9.30am-6pm Mon-Sat, to 9pm Thu, 11am-5pm Sun 🚇 St James Ⓜ City Centre

Orson & Blake (6, E5) See p59.

Zomp (5, D6) The shoes here are great, with chic imports (Costume National) and the less pricey, just as wearable house label. Whatever the shoe of the season – pointy, bubble-toed, high-heeled or strappy – Zomp will have it and so can you.
☎ 9221 4027 ✉ L1, Mid City Centre, 197 Pitt St Mall 🕙 9am-6pm Mon-Fri, to 9pm Thu, 9am-5pm Sat, 11am-5pm Sun 🚇 St James Ⓜ City Centre

Mambo in da house

MUSIC & BOOKS

ABC Shop (5, D7) The ABC (or 'Auntie' as it's lovingly known) appeals to a broad range of tastes and age groups, and so does their bookshop. Kids love the wall of videos, books and sing-along tapes; teenagers buy cult TV T-shirts and comedy videos; adults stock up on arts videos, classical music recordings and high-brow coffee-table books.
☎ 9286 3726 🖳 www .abc.net.au ✉ Shop 48, L1, Queen Victoria Building, 455 George St ⏱ 9am-5.30pm Mon-Fri, to 8pm Thu, 9am-5pm Sat, 11am-5pm Sun 🚉 Town Hall Ⓜ Galeries Victoria 🚌 George St buses

Ariel (6, B4) Artists, photographers, architects and students roam Ariel's aisles by day and late into the night. 'Underculture' is the thrust here – there are hundreds of glossy art, film, fashion and design books, along with kids books, travel guides and the queer literature section. Browse for a while before a movie at the Verona or Academy Twin cinemas across the road.
☎ 9332 45812 🖳 www .arielbooks.com.au ✉ 42 Oxford St, Paddington ⏱ 9am-midnight 🚌 378, 380, 382, L82

Berkelouw Books (6, B4) Expecting the dank aroma of musty second-hand books? Forget about it! Follow your nose up the spiral staircase to the café for a fix, then browse down through three floors of pre-loved tomes,

new releases, antique maps and Australia's largest collection of rare books.
☎ 9360 3200 🖳 www .berkelouw.com.au ✉ 19 Oxford St, Paddington ⏱ 9am-midnight 🚌 378, 380, 382, L82

Bookshop (6, B4) This large gay and lesbian bookshop in the throbbing shaft of the Oxford St Golden Mile has got all the bases covered. Titles range from queer theory through to erotica and Australian fiction.
☎ 9331 1103 🖳 www .thebookshop.com.au ✉ 207 Oxford St, Darlinghurst ⏱ 10am-10pm Mon-Wed, to 11pm Thu, 11am-midnight Fri-Sat, to 11pm Sun 🚌 378, 380, 382, L82

Central Station (6, A3) Clubbers, DJs and dance music aficionados descend the stairs into this basement store to pick up the latest local and overseas releases. Techno, hip-hop, trance and house music dominate. Dance-party tickets, imported magazines and streetwear (Milkfed, X-Large, Sur) also make the grade.
☎ 9361 5222 🖳 www .centralstationrec.com ✉ 14 Oxford St, Darlinghurst ⏱ 10am-7pm Mon-Fri, to 9pm Thu, to 6pm Sat, noon-6pm Sun 🚉 Museum 🚌 378, 380, 382, L82

Folkways (6, D5) If Mongolian throat singers rock your world, then long-established

Gleebooks: gleeful reads

Folkways – the city's premier stockist of world music CDs – is your spiritual home. Expect pressings from central Asia to the central Australian desert and an extensive selection of jazz and blues.
☎ 9361 3980 🖳 info@folkways.com .au ✉ 282 Oxford St, Paddington ⏱ 9am-6pm Mon-Sat, to 9pm Thu, 11am-6pm Sun 🚌 378, 380, 382, L82

Gleebooks (2, B4) Gleebooks – a ramshackle two-storey terrace house – is widely regarded as Sydney's best bookshop. The aisles are packed with an eclectic mix of politics, arts and general fiction and staff know their stuff backwards. Its annual literary programme attracts big-name local (Winton, Leunig etc) and international authors. The childrens and second-hand bookshop is at 191 Glebe Point Rd.
☎ 9660 2333 🖳 www .gleebooks.com.au ✉ 49 Glebe Point Rd, Glebe ⏱ 9am-9pm 🚌 431-4

HMV (5, D6) This Brit global megachain has set up shop in most of the world's big cities – Sydney's no exception. The top-40, commercial dance and cult DVD sections are balanced by a comprehensive classical, blues and world-music room next door. They also stock vinyl and singles. His master's voice never sounded so complex. ☎ 9221 2311 ☐ www .hmv.com.au ✉ LG, Mid City Centre, 197 Pitt St Mall ☽ 8.30am-7pm Mon-Fri, to 9pm Thu, 9.30am-6pm Sat, 10.30am-5.30pm Sun ☒ St James Ⓜ City Centre

Kinokuniya (5, D7) Wrapping around the Galeries Victoria (TGV) atrium, Kinokuniya has over 300,000 titles on one level and confidently claims to be the largest bookstore in Sydney.

The comics section is a magnet for geeky teens; the imported Chinese, Japanese and European magazine section isn't. Ogle the extensive music and architecture shelves then hit the café. ☎ 9262 7996 ☐ www .kinokuniya.com ✉ L3, The Galeries Victoria, 500 George St ☽ 10am-7pm Mon-Sat, to 9pm Thu, 10am-6pm Sun ☒ Town Hall Ⓜ Galeries Victoria ☒ George St buses

Martin Smith's Bookshop (3, B2) Do bushy-bushy blonde surfies and tourists read books? If the crowds at Martin Smith's are anything to go by, the answer must be yes. This tiny cultural oasis in Bondi's literary desert has more books than space – staff scramble up and down wooden ladders to get to the top shelves.

☎ 9365 1482 ☐ www .martinsmithbooks.com .au ✉ 3 Hall St, Bondi Beach ☽ 10am-9.30pm ☒ 380, 389 or L82 from Circular Quay, 381-2 from Bondi Junction

Virgin Megastore (5, D5) See **HMV** above... No, seriously, as Dick Branson would attest, Virgin do enough things differently to warrant their own listing. And even if you don't buy anything here, it's worth a visit just for a squiz at the amazing old banking chambers now counting the dollars of mainstream rock 'n' roll. ☎ 9347 0300 ☐ www .virgin.com.au ✉ 343 George St ☽ 8.30am-7pm Mon-Wed, to 9pm Thu, to 8pm Fri, 9am-6pm Sat, 10am-6pm Sun ☒ Martin Place ☒ George St buses

Bookish Sydney

Scan the shelves for the following Sydney-centric reads:

- *The Bodysurfers*, Robert Drewe (1983) Seductive stories from Bondi to the Northern Beaches.
- *Bombora*, Tegan Bennett (1996) Tight Coogee fiction.
- *Camille's Bread*, Amanda Lohrey (1995) Postmodern love in Glebe, Leichhardt and Chinatown.
- *He Died with a Felafel in His Hand*, John Birmingham (1994) Beer, bongs and cockroaches.
- *The Cross*, Mandy Sayer (1995) Sleazy '70s Kings Cross murder.
- *The Glass Canoe*, David Ireland (1976) Sydney's amber-hued pub culture.
- *The Harp in the South* and *Poor Man's Orange*, Ruth Park (1948 & 1949) Impoverished family life in Surry Hills.
- *The Last Magician*, Janette Turner Hospital (1992) Seedy corruption around Newtown Station.
- *Lilian's Story*, Kate Grenville (1985) The life of Sydney eccentric Bea Miles.
- *The Service of Clouds*, Delia Falconer (1997) Blue Mountains magic realism and capital 'R' romance.
- *Unreliable Memoirs*, Clive James (1980) Boy-Clive in Sydney's southern 'burbs.
- *Voss*, Patrick White (1957) The unforgiving outback versus Sydney's colonial life.

FOOD & DRINK

Cyril's Fine Foods (5, C9)
Cyril's is an old-style deli stocking 4000 different product lines, mainly European smallgoods, chocolates, cheeses, mustards and variously pickled things. Cyril Vincent has opened his store at the crack of dawn for almost 50 years – Dawn doesn't seem to mind, and his loyal customers keep coming back for his nongourmet prices.
☎ 9211 0994 ✉ 181 Hay St, Haymarket ⏱ 6am-5pm Mon-Fri, to 1pm Sat 🚉 Central Ⓜ Powerhouse Museum 🚉 Capitol Square 🚌 George St buses

David Jones Food Hall (5, D6)
This prestigious food hall is wont to overwhelm the senses: noses assail chunks of cheese and bins of coffee, eyes flutter at fresh seafood and antipasto, mouths drool uncontrollably over choice pastries and sushi. Your hip pocket mightn't be as keen on the whole deal as your body.
☎ 9266 5544 🖥 www .davidjones.com ✉ LG, 66-77 Market St ⏱ 9.30am-6pm Mon-Fri, to 9pm Thu, 9am-6pm Sat, 11am-5pm Sun 🚉 St James Ⓜ City Centre

Fox Studio's Farmers Market (2, D5)
Line your coffers with fresh farm produce: free-range eggs and poultry, organic meat, fruit and vegetables, flowers, fish and pastries. The kids can run free and wild at the adjacent playground while you snack on home-made *pirozhki* and danishes.
☎ 9383 4163 🖥 www .foxstudios.com.au /markets/farmers.asp ✉ Driver Ave, Moore Park ⏱ 10am-5pm Wed, to 4pm Sat 🚌 371-4, 376-7 Ⓟ 2hr free

Good Living Grower's Market (5, A6)
This picturesque, foodies market showcases the best regional produce in NSW. Stroll through the 90 stalls and poke at all sorts of delicacies from goat's cheese and sourdough bread to smoked tuna and wattleseed ice cream. Grab a coffee and reconstitute with an egg, bacon and chutney roll.
☎ 9282 3606 🖥 www .events.smh.com.au ✉ Pyrmont Bay Park, Pirrama Rd, Pyrmont ⏱ 7-11am 1st Sat of each month (not Jan) Ⓜ Harbourside 🚉 🚢 Pyrmont Bay

Jones The Grocer (6, E5)
High-end groceries, cookbooks and a café for breakfast and lunch gourmet goodies. Hoe into a caramel slice with a strong coffee, then raid the cheese room. Make sure the creamy double brie is double-wrapped then hotfoot it to Centennial Park for a picnic.
☎ 9362 1222 🖥 www .jonesthegrocer.com.au ✉ 68 Moncur St, Woollahra ⏱ 8.30am-6.30pm Mon-Fri, to 5.30pm Sat, to 5pm Sun 🚌 378, 380, 382, 389, L82

La Gerbe d'Or (6, D4)
Possibly Sydney's most-loved patisserie, La Gerbe d'Or (pron: with *theek* Parisian accent) has been baking mouth-watering French breads, cakes, pastries and quiches for more than 20 years. The chunky beef burgundy pies they sell here are legendary.
☎ 9331 1070 🖥 www

There's something fishy going on at Sydney Fish Market

.lagerbedor.net ✉ 255 Glenmore Rd, Five Ways, Paddington 🕙 8am-7pm Tue-Fri, to 4pm Sat, to 1pm Sun 🚌 378, 380, 382, 389, L82

Macro (2, D5) The staff here are herbal and humming, massaging each other's shoulders in between stocking the shelves. New Age music lilts softly as shoppers buy rainforest honey, herbal tea and organic fruit and veg. There's a cool café, juice bar and homeopathic dispensary on site if the vibe takes you.
☎ 9389 7611
💻 www.macrowhole foods.com.au ✉ 31-5 Oxford St, Bondi Junction 🕙 8am-8pm Mon-Fri, to 7pm Sat, 9am-7pm Sun 🚈 Bondi Junction 🚌 378, 380, 382, 389, L82

Max Brenner (6, D5) 'Chocolate by the Bald Man' is Max Brenner's catch-cry. No chance of finding any stray follicles in your Ghanaian hot chocolate (the strongest variety available). Still craving? Try a handful of pralines, a pound of pralines or Max's signature 'Sukao' drink (thick milk chocolate warmed over a tea-light candle).
☎ 9357 5055 💻 www .maxbrenner.com ✉ 447 Oxford St, Paddington 🕙 10am-6.30pm Mon-Sat, 11am-6.30pm Sun 🚌 378, 380, 382, L82

Pompei's (3, B1) Lushly folded gelati is doled out in pastel-coloured plastic

Jones the Grocer, Bob the Builder.

cups (which are too good to throw away). Choose from over 20 flavours, all made with real cream, milk and organic fruit. The 'Crème Caramel' and milky 'Fior di Latte' are sublime.
☎ 9365 1233; fax 9365 1244 ✉ cnr Roscoe & Gould Sts, Bondi Beach 🕙 11am-late Tue-Sat 🚌 380, 389 or L82 from Circular Quay, 381-2 from Bondi Junction

Simon Johnson (6, E6) The sun's out and the beach is beckoning; a Simon Johnson hamper of luxurious morsels is what you need (Italian olives, French cheeses, organic biscuits, Belgian chocolates, mango nectar and truffles). Ask about the talk/eat/drink classes they run with local and international culinary gurus.
☎ 9328 6888 💻 www .simonjohnson.com.au ✉ 55 Queen St, Woollahra 🕙 10.30am-7pm Mon-Fri, 9am-5pm Sat, 10am-4pm Sun 🚌 378, 380, 382, 389, L82

Sydney Fish Market (2, B4) Chefs, locals and overfed seagulls haggle over mud crabs, Balmain bugs and lobsters at Sydney's No 1 fish market. This piscatorial precinct on Blackwattle Bay has retailers, restaurants, a marina, seafood school, early morning auctions and auction tours (call for info).
☎ 9660 1611 💻 www .sydneyfishmarket.com. au ✉ Bank St, Pyrmont 🕙 7am-4pm 🚈 Fish Market 🚌 501, 443 Ⓟ

Ultimo Wine Centre (5, B9) Sydney's leading import specialist, with wines divided regionally and special sections devoted to books and boozy accessories. A regular newsletter sounds the upcoming shipment and discount alarm. The well-timed Saturday-afternoon wine tasting draws a crowd.
☎ 9211 2380 ✉ 99 Jones St, Ultimo 🕙 9am-7pm Mon-Wed, to 8pm Thu & Fri, 10am-8pm Sat, 11am-4pm Sun
🚈 🚉 Central 🚌 501

JEWELLERY & ACCESSORIES

Dinosaur Designs (6, D5)
If Fred and Barney opened a jewellery store, this is exactly what it would look like. Oversized, jewel-coloured, translucent resin bangles and baubles sit among technicoloured vases and bowls and chunky sterling-silver rings and necklaces.
☎ 9361 3776 🖵 www
.dinosaurdesigns.com.au
✉ 339 Oxford St, Paddington ◔ 10am-6pm
Mon-Sat, noon-5pm Sun
🚌 378, 380, 382, L82

Love & Hatred (5, D6) This plush, sensual, wood-panelled store is aglow with custom-made jewellery by Sydney designer Giovanni D'ercole. His beautiful sapphire rings, natural pearls and rose-gold pieces manifest a striking, effortless blend of Celtic, Art Nouveau and contemporary styles without ostentatiousness.
☎ 9233 3441 🖵 www
.loveandhatred.com.au
✉ L1, Strand Arcade,
412 George St ◔ 10am-5.30pm Mon-Fri, to 8pm Thu, to 4.30pm Sat
🚊 Town Hall Ⓜ City Centre 🚌 George St buses

Oroton (5, D6) Oroton vends sophisticated leathers in a select palette of colours: black, red and tan. Wallets, handbags, belts, shoes, cufflinks and Jackie O-style sunglasses all have the air of instant classics.
☎ 9223 2449 🖵 www
.oroton.com.au ✉ Shop 1A, 183 Pitt St Mall
◔ 9am-6pm Mon-Fri, to 9pm Thu, 11am-5pm Sat 🚊 St James, Martin Place Ⓜ City Centre

Paspaley Pearls (5, D6)
This shell-shaped store sells lustrous South Sea pearls the size of your eyeball set in classic and modern designs. Prices start at $450 for a ring and rise to more than $1 million for a hefty strand of perfect pink pearls.
☎ 9232 7633 🖵 www
.paspaleypearls.
com ✉ 142 King St
◔ 9.30am-6pm Mon-Fri, 11am-5pm Sat 🚊 St James, Martin Place
Ⓜ City Centre

Vern Jewels (6, B4) With an exquisite eye and a wry sense of history, Nicholas Bullough (no, he's not Vern, that's a joke – Jules Verne, get it?) assembles the artefacts, stones, pearls and gems he buys around the world and comes up with winners every time.
☎ 9361 3669 ✉ 36B Oxford St, Paddington
◔ 10am-5pm Mon-Sat
🚌 378, 380, 382, L82

Victoria Spring (6, C4)
Paddington princesses head to this super-salon to procure delicately beaded, vintage-style costume jewellery. Equally delectable crystal chandeliers, embroidered satin bedspreads and delicate china teapots complete the femme-fatale fantasy.
☎ 9331 7862 🖵 www
.victoriaspringdesigns.
com.au ✉ 110 Oxford St, Paddington ◔ 10am-6pm Mon-Sat, to 7pm Thu, 1-5pm Sun 🚌 378, 380, 382, L82

All That Glitters
Five stand out Sydney jewellers, comin' atcha like Cleopatra:
Anne Schofield (6, E5; ☎ 9363 1326; www.anne schofieldantiques.com; 36 Queen St, Woollahra) Antique jewellery for those lucky enough to have a huge trust fund.
Fairfax & Roberts (5, D5; www.fairfaxandroberts .com.au; ☎ 9232 8511; 44 Martin Pl) Classy, classy, classy… A night at the opera?
Gemtec (5, D4; ☎ 9251 1599; www.gemtec. com.au; 51 Pitt St) Australian gems and high security.
Hardy Brothers (5, D6; ☎ 9232 2422; www.har dybrothers.com.au; 77 Castlereagh St) Establishment jewellery for your country estate.
Tiffany & Co (5, D5; ☎ 9235 1777; 39 Martin Pl) Trinkets in cute boxes.

ANTIQUES & HOMEWARES

Antiques? Head to Queen St, Woollahra without delay. The CBD department stores and shopping centres are your best bet for homewares, but if city traffic (mechanical and human) isn't what you feel like, here is a handful of other options.

Architectural Heritage (2, B5) Take a trip into this strange world of suspended history and architectural salvage genius. To the tune of piped Gatsby-era swing, the grumpily eccentric management lets you explore two jam-packed levels of babbling fountains, stained-glass windows, wrought-iron balustrades, marble hearths, bronze sculptures, urns, staircases and figureheads from places entirely elsewhere and more mysterious.
☎ 9660 0100 ✉ 62 **Glebe Point Rd, Glebe** 🕑 10am-6pm 🚌 431-4

Arte Flowers (6, E5) Part florist, part gift shop, part tea rooms, this airy space carries French perfume and skincare products, delicate bead earrings, chic gardening tools and serves afternoon tea around its communal table. After all that shopping you deserve a cup of orange-blossom tea and a slice of lemon tart.
☎ 9328 0402; fax 9328 6122 ✉ 112 Queen St, **Woollahra** 🕑 10am-5.30pm Mon-Fri, 9.30am-5.30pm Sat, 10am-5pm Sun 🚌 378, 380, 382, 389, L82

Caravan (3, B1) The luxe-hippy look perfected – if it's beaded, ruched or ruffled you'll find it in this exotic little shop. North African tea glasses, embroidered quilts made from Indian wedding saris, kimonos, deck chairs and etched mirrors. Fellas, if it all looks a bit pink and girly, go and play with the wicked carved double-domed Moroccan lanterns.
☎ 9365 0500 ✉ 85 Hall **St, Bondi Beach** 🕑 11am-6pm 🚌 380, 389 or L82 **from Circular Quay, 381-2 from Bondi Junction**

Orson & Blake (6, E5) Sydney's most stylin' home-wares emporium will make your house look cool even if you're not – everything from notepads to garden statues at the height of chic. Head upstairs for clothes by top-notch Australian and Kiwi designers plus opulent scarves, handbags and jewellery.
☎ 9326 1155 💻 orsblake@zipworld

.com.au ✉ 83-5 Queen St, Woollahra 🕑 9.30am-5.30pm Mon-Sat, noon-5pm Sun 🚌 378, 380, 382, 389, L82

Sydney Antique Centre (6, B5) Sydney's oldest antique shop, the capacious Sydney Antique Centre has over 60 dealers specialising in porcelain, silver, glass, collectables and furniture. Items range from sports memorabilia to antique grandfather clocks to Art Deco jewellery. Pick up a 19th-century alabaster mannequin or an ornate bronze Parisian urn then drag them 'round the café and bookshop.
☎ 9361 3244 💻 www .sydantcent.com.au ✉ 531 South Dowling St, **Surry Hills** 🕑 10am-6pm 🚌 339, 340, 373, 374, 390-4

Antique Critique

Queen St, Woollahra is the hub of Sydney's antique trade. If you're in the market for an old-time souvenir of your visit, look for early Australian colonial furniture made from cedar or Huon Pine (aka Yellow Gold), Australian silver jewellery (either early factory or studio ceramic pieces, especially anything by the Boyd family), glassware (such as Carnival glass) and collectable Australiana paraphernalia like old signs, tins, bottles.

Updated annually, *Carter's Price Guide to Antiques in Australia* is an excellent reference. Also have a look at the free quarterly *Antiques In New South Wales*.

AUSTRALIAN GOODS

Australian Geographic Store (5, D6) Croaking frogs and chirping cicadas resonate in the background as you roam this store. You can't buy a frog, but there are plenty of Australiana gifts and gadgets with a scientific and environmental bent. Or would Sir like some silk Australian-flag boxer shorts? ☎ 9221 8299 💻 www .ausgeo.com.au ✉ Sydney Arcade, Pitt St Mall ⏰ 9am-6pm Mon-Fri, to 9pm Thu, to 5pm Sat, 11am-4pm Sun 🚉 St James Ⓜ City Centre

Australian Wine Centre (5, D4) This small multilingual basement store is packed with quality Australian wine, beer and spirits. Pick up some Yellowglen for a bubbly night or organise a shipment of Ninth Island Pinot Noir back home. Rotund wallets access the Cuban cigar

Ken Done condoned

humidor and a swaggering range of Penfold's Grange wines. ☎ 9247 2755 💻 www .australianwinecentre .com ✉ Shop 3, Goldfields House, 1 Alfred St, Circular Quay ⏰ 9.30am-7pm Mon-Wed & Sat, to 8pm Thu & Fri, to 6.30pm Sun 🚉 🚌 🚢 Circular Quay

Done Art & Design (5, D3) Ken Done is like George Michael — he peaked in the '80s but he just won't go away. The sunny side of Australiana, his optimistic, colourful images of Sydney icons are primed for the tourist market. They're emblazoned on everything from T-shirts to drink coasters to handbags. Strewth Ken, not another Opera House mouse-pad… ☎ 9251 6099 💻 www .done.com.au ✉ 123-5 George St, The Rocks ⏰ 10am-6pm 🚉 🚌 🚢 Circular Quay

Ken Duncan Gallery (5, D3) Saturated with colour and light, Duncan's Australian landscape photos make amateur photographers bristle with envy. Uluru, Opera House and outback all get the Duncan treatment. Limited-edition prints are pricey, but you can buy his work in book, calendar, gift-card, DVD or video format. ☎ 9241 3460 💻 www .kenduncan.com ✉ 73 George St, The Rocks ⏰ 9am-7pm 🚉 🚌 🚢 Circular Quay

Naturally Australian (5, D3) This converted 1880s steamship warehouse blooms with the work of over 50 Australian timber designers. Jarrah jewellery boxes, Huon pine platters, Sassafras salt- and peppershakers and myrtle chessboards are as pleasing in the hand as they are to the eye. ☎ 9247 1531 💻 www .naturallyaust.com.au ✉ 43 Circular Quay West, The Rocks ⏰ 9.30am-5.30pm 🚉 🚌 🚢 Circular Quay

Opal Fields (5, D4) Follow the red carpet from the footpath to a glittering array of Australian opals in a gallery-style store. Bottom of the market is a pair of solid opal earrings for $60. A black opal pendant may put you thousands in the red. ☎ 9247 6800 💻 www .opalfields.com ✉ 190 George St, The Rocks ⏰ 9am-6pm 🚉 🚌 🚢 Circular Quay

RM Williams (5, D6) Urban cowboys, country folk and tourists make a beeline for this hardwearing outback gear. It's the kind of stuff politicians don when they want to seem 'fair dinkum' about something. Prime ministerial favourites include oilskin jackets, Akubra hats, moleskin jeans and tough leather work boots. ☎ 9262 2228 💻 www .rmwilliams.com .au ✉ 389 George St

⌚ 8.30am-6pm Mon-Fri, to 8.30pm Thu, 9am-5pm Sat, 11am-5pm Sun
🚉 Wynyard, Town Hall Ⓜ City Centre
🚌 George St buses

Strand Hatters (5, D6)

Got a cold/wet head? Strand Hatters will cover your crown with a classically Australian Akubra bush hat (made from rabbit felt), a beret, bowler or a Monte Cristo 'Gambler' panama. The staff will block and steam hats to customer requirements and provide crocodile-teeth hatbands for a small extra fee.
☎ 9231 6884 🖥 www.strandhatters.com.au
✉ Strand Arcade, 412 George St ⌚ 8.30am-6pm Mon-Fri, to 8pm Thu, 9.30am-4.30pm Sat, 11am-4pm Sun 🚉 Town Hall Ⓜ City Centre
🚌 George St buses

Opals

Opals, Australia's national gemstones, are magnificently coloured stones formed over time by percolating ground waters. Their incandescent, shimmering displays come in many varieties from jelly (transparent with flashes of colour) to black (dark body colour enhanced by other shades). Opals make an appropriately 'Oz' gift whether you're visiting Sydney or just want some beauty in your life. Prices depend on flaws and the brilliance of colour, but expect to pay between $50 and $3000. Head for the duty-free shops and jewellers in The Rocks and QVB.

Wilderness Society Shop (5, D6)

The non-profit Wilderness Society campaigns for the preservation of Australia's rainforests and waterways. Its store stocks unusual and reasonably priced gifts – lemon-myrtle tea, recycled timber windchimes, picture frames, books and essential oils – and smells amazing (it's the organ oil that's been rubbed into the floorboards).
☎ 9233 4674 🖥 www.wilderness.org.au
✉ Shop C3, Castlereagh St Level, Centrepoint ⌚ 9am-6pm Mon-Fri, to 8pm Thu, to 5pm Sat, 10am-5pm Sun 🚉 St James Ⓜ City Centre

Is that John Howard in the picture? Go see for yourself at RM Williams.

SHOPPING FOR KIDS

Circus Bizurcus (6, G3)
If the nanny's taken ill and you have to look after the little buggers yourself, bring them here. They'll adore you for buying them a kid-size 12V two-speed silver Porsche 911 with rubber tyres and electrically assisted brakes (imported from Milan). Now *that's* good parenting... ☎ 9362 0183; fax 9362 0794 ✉ Shop 9, 19-27 Cross St, Double Bay ☯ 9.30am-5.30pm Mon-Sat, 11am-5pm Sun 🚆 Edgecliff then 🚌 323-6, L24 ⛴ Double Bay

Fragile (6, E5) Dress your fragile Little Lord Fauntleroy in expensive kids labels like Petit Bateau, Paul Smith, Quincy, Da Da, Ma Muse and Hakka. They sell handmade soft toys, contemporary cots, embroidered bed linen and ultra-sturdy buggies too. Also at Chifley Plaza. ☎ 9362 0085 🖳 www .fragile.com.au ✉ 76a

Paddington St, Paddington ☯ 10am-5.30pm Mon-Sat, to 7pm Thu, 11am-5pm Sun 🚌 378, 380, 382, L82

Hobbyco (5, D6) Run by hobbyists for people who take their fun seriously, Hobbyco's aisles fill with excited boys (big and small) effusing over slot cars, Meccano sets, Hornby trains and radio-controlled cars like the kick-arse Audi TT jigsaw puzzles with 12,000 pieces and First Fleet models are perfect projects for a rainy year. ☎ 9221 0666 🖳 www .hobbyco.com.au ✉ Shop 402, Gallery Level, Mid City Centre, Pitt St Mall ☯ 9am-6pm Mon-Sat, to 9pm Thu, 11am-5pm Sun 🚆 St James Ⓜ City Centre

Kidstuff (6, F5) Parents seem relieved to discover this small store filled with educational, traditional, low-

tech toys and games. Aiming to engage and expand kids' minds, well-known brands mix with costumes, musical instruments, soft toys, dolls houses and magnetic fridge letters (teach them how to spell 'p-l-a-y-s-t-a-t-i-o-n'). ☎ 9363 2838; fax 9363 9210 ✉ 126a Queen St, Woollahra ☯ 9.30am-5.30pm Mon-Fri, to 5pm Sat, 9am-4pm Sun 🚌 378, 380, 382, 389, L82

Puppet Shop at The Rocks (5, D3) Puppet master Phillip (all the way from the Belgian Congo) beguiles you with his accent as you 'enter the dazzling caves of wonders'. Dangling from the ceiling of his sandstone cellar are hundreds of incredible handmade wizards, skeletons, soldiers, jesters and spooky Chinese puppets from $100 to $500. I'd hate to come here at night... ☎ 9247 9137 🖳 www .thepuppetshop.com ✉ 77 George St, The Rocks ☯ 10am-5pm 🚆 🚌 ⛴ Circular Quay

Sticky (5, D3) Take the kids to see thick, technicolour swirls of lollipop, toffee and boiled-sweet sugars being stirred up in vats, rolled out on tables and pummelled into shape by pugilistic sugar daddies (these boys don't muck around). Chew on a bag of caramels and ponder a career change. ☎ 9252 3337 🖳 www .sticky.com.au ✉ Shop 17, The Rocks Centre ☯ 9am-6pm 🚆 🚌 ⛴ Circular Quay

---

Your Duty to Save

Prices for duty-free items compare favourably with the rest of the world but remember that ordinary store prices may be cheaper. Shop around before you buy. Duty-free shops abound in the city; here are four of the best:

DFS Galleria (5, D4; ☎ 8243 8666; www.dfsgalleria.com; 155 George St, The Rocks)

Downtown Duty Free (5, D6; ☎ 9233 3166; www.dutyfree.com.au; Basement, Strand Arcade, 412 George St)

Fletchers Fotographics (5, D7; ☎ 9267 6146; www.fletchers.net; 317-9 Pitt St)

Harbourside (5, D6; ☎ 9283 8900; fax 9253 8950; 249 Pitt St)

Eating

Other Australian cities hate to admit it, but Sydney has won the food trifecta. Its multicultural melange, abundant fresh produce and geographic assets make it a superb place to eat. Adelaide may have the great wines, Melbourne the café culture and Hobart the seafood, but Sydney has it all, right on Sydney Harbour.

Restaurants hum and as inner-city gentrification continues, more and more corner pubs are transforming into brasseries, bookshops are installing espresso machines and locals are finding their own kitchens increasingly wearisome.

Sydney Cuisine

Modern Australian cuisine (Mod Oz) continues to evolve as chefs consult Asia for ingredients and Europe for technique. Cooking focuses on fresh, healthy eating, drawing on rich and diverse migrant community influences.

At the top end, celebrity chefs plate up mini-masterpieces for wealthy corporate crowds. Those on tighter budgets need not despair; thousands of cafés, bistros and restaurants offer innovative, quality meals at moderate prices. In this chapter, restaurants with good or wholly vegetarian selections are marked with the **V** icon, 'options' indicating fewer choices.

Liquor & Smoking

Licensing laws in Sydney are gradually being modernised. For the moment though, most licensed restaurants can't serve patrons alcohol unless they order a meal. Most restaurants have a good wine list, pushing Australian product. Restaurant prices are more expensive than in bottle shops, ranging from $25 to $50 per bottle – a decent drop will set you back about $30. Wine sold by the glass is also widely available. You can bring your own alcohol to BYO restaurants – see p65 for details.

Smoking is banned in all restaurants, cafés and in the dining areas of pubs and bars.

Meal Costs

The price ranges in this chapter use the $ symbol to indicate the cost of a two-course meal for one person, excluding alcohol. Many eateries charge a 10% surcharge on weekends and public holidays.

$	$20 and under
$$	$21-49
$$$	$50-79
$$$$	$80 and over

Bather's Pavilion, Balmoral

Opening Hours

Cafés and restaurants are generally open seven days, with many cafés serving food from 7am to 10pm. Most restaurants are open for lunch and dinner, while cafés and patisseries are the best bet for breakfast. Bookings are required at the more expensive restaurants, especially for dinner.

BONDI & BRONTE

To get to Bondi Beach and North Bondi catch bus 380, 389 or L82 from Circular Quay or 381-2 from Bondi Junction. For Bronte take bus 378 from Bondi Junction or Railway Sq.

Bondi Icebergs (3, B2) $$$
Modern Mediterranean
This restaurant has one of the most beautiful locations in Sydney, with a stunning outlook over the arc of Bondi Beach – diners have sensational views. The seafood is fresh and cooked with élan, the wine list superb, and the bar's never a boring place for a beer.
☎ 9365 9000 🖳 www .idrb.com ✉ 1 Notts Ave, Bondi 🕒 noon-midnight Tue-Sat, to 10pm Sun

Brio (3, A3) $$
Mod Oz
Brio is brilliant when its French doors open to the spectacular beach views. Just as dazzling is the made-to-share tasting plate: delicious morsels of wild mushrooms, yam and truffle spring rolls and skewered grilled scallops

Sean's Panaroma

are lip-smackingly good. The handmade Balmain bug and crab ravioli is also a treat.
☎ 9369 3227 🖳 www .briobrontebeach.com.au ✉ 467 Bronte Rd, Bronte 🕒 7am-10pm Ⓥ & vegan

Brown Sugar (3, C1) $
Café
Act like a local and rock up for big afternoon breakfasts under the glow of Brown Sugar's cherry walls. Order the signature 'black stone eggs' (poached eggs, bacon, oven-roasted tomatoes and cheese on an English muffin) and keep an eye out for Jack Johnson or Flea from the Red Hot Chilli Peppers.
☎ 9365 6262 🖳 brown sugarcafe@hotmail.com ✉ 100 Brighton Blvd, North Bondi 🕒 7.30am-4pm Mon-Fri, 8am-4pm Sat & Sun ♿ Ⓥ

Gelbison (3, B2) $
Italian
Legendary to the point where there's a local rock band named after it, Gelbison entertains families, backpackers, locals and visiting movie stars with great-value pizza and pasta. Sit with the surfers over a steaming bowl of mussel fettuccine or a flying saucer–sized pizza.
☎ 9130 4042; fax 9300 9041 ✉ 10 Lamrock Ave, Bondi 🕒 5-11pm ♿ Ⓥ options

Gertrude & Alice (3, B1) $
Café
This second-hand book-shop/café is so un-Bondi; there's not a model or surfer in sight. Locals, students and academics hang out all day reading, drinking coffee and acting like Americans in Paris. Join them for a mezze platter and theological discussion around com-munal tables in shambolic book-lined rooms.
☎ /fax 9130 5155 ✉ 40 Hall St, Bondi 🕒 9.30am-11pm Mon & Tue, to midnight Wed-Fri, 8.30am-midnight Sat & Sun Ⓥ

Jackies (3, C1) $$$
Mod Oz
Jackies has a cool interior and cooler clientele – DJs, maga-zine editors and film makers malinger, sucking inspiration from the proto-industrial artefacture and killer views up and down Bondi Beach. Ignore them. Freshly shucked Sydney rock oysters, blue swimmer crab linguini and crispy-skin Atlantic salmon are more interesting.
☎ 9300 9812 🖳 www .jackies-restaurant-and -bar.com ✉ 132 Warn-ers Ave, North Bondi 🕒 noon-midnight Mon-Fri, 8am-midnight Sat & Sun

Jed's Foodstore (3, B1) $
Café
Jed's is so relaxed, you'll feel like you're living in a

uni share house again. Reggae mellows the tattooed staff, who sing and groove around. Dudes sip coffee on milk crates outside as kids and dogs run amuck. Grab a seat for the spiced-ricotta pancakes with berry compote and maple syrup.

☎ 9365 0022 ✉ **cnr Glenayr & Warners Aves, North Bondi** 🕑 **6.30am-6pm Mon-Fri, 8am-6pm Sat & Sun** 🚼 Ⓥ

Moorish (3, C1) $$$
Modern Moroccan/ Mediterranean
Moorish's huge plate-glass windows float above the lift and sigh of the North Bondi swell. You won't be able to hear any sighs inside (there's a lot of hard surfaces) but the food will occupy all your other senses. The roasted clams with Manzanilla sherry, capsicum, couscous and lemon are definite show-stoppers.

☎ 9300 9511 🖳 www .moorishrestaurant.com .au ✉ **118-20 Ramsgate Ave, North Bondi** 🕑 **noon-3pm & 6-11pm Mon-Fri, 10am-4pm & 6-11pm Sat & Sun, to 9.30pm Sun**

Mu Shu (3, B2) $$$
Modern Asian
A cream and dark chocolate interior enshrouds Mu Shu's 9m oak bar, private booths, communal tables, Chinese screens, fish tanks and duck-roasting oven. The architects went to town, but you can enjoy yum cha or slow-cooked ocean trout with olives, saffron, fennel,

Bring Your Own
Many restaurants advertise themselves as BYO. This means you can Bring Your Own alcohol, though you'll generally be charged a corkage fee ($2 to $5 per bottle, sometimes per person). Most BYO eateries are unlicensed, but some licensed places also allow you to BYO – this may be restricted to bottled wine only.

and papaya without leaving the beach.

☎ 9130 5400 🖳 www .mushu.com.au ✉ **108 Campbell Pde, Bondi** 🕑 **noon-3pm Thu-Sun, 6pm-midnight daily**

Sean's Panaroma (3, C1) $$$
Mod Oz
Ocean views, creative dishes, friendly staff and celebrity attendees ensure this hip little noshery's fame. With an ever-changing menu, Sean lets you eat with the seasons. Suckling pig roasted with cabbage, pear, sweet potato and anise is a winter night's feast. In summer, succumb to seafood.

☎ 9365 4924 🖳 www .seanspanaroma.com.au ✉ **270 Campbell Pde, North Bondi** 🕑 **noon-3pm Sat & Sun, 6.30-9.30pm Wed-Sat**

Sejuiced (3, A3) $
Café
This seduction is subtle. First, they give you a sunny footpath table with ocean views and plenty of beachy soul. Next comes a virtuous 'morning energiser' juice (beetroot, apple, ginger, carrot). By the time your caffeine-hit kicks in, you're well and truly Sejuiced.

☎ 9389 9538 ✉ **487**

Bronte Rd, Bronte 🕑 **6.30am-6.30pm** 🚼 Ⓥ

Swell (3, A3) $$
Mod Oz
At the end of Bronte's breezy row of eateries, Swell has a spanking day-turns to night menu. Greet the day with poached eggs, pumpkin, feta and spinach, linger into lunch with a snazzy steak sandwich and return at dinnertime for the salt-and-pepper squid.

☎ 9386 5001 🖳 www .swellrestaurant.com .au ✉ **465 Bronte Rd, Bronte** 🕑 **7am-10pm** Ⓥ **options**

Trio (3, B2) $$
Mod Oz
Covering the bases from breakfast to cocktails, Trio surfs the southern hip of Bondi's curve, quickly building a name as one of the beach's best (*oooh*, is that Mark and Delta in the corner?). Try the vanilla-scented french toast for breakfast or the seafood grill as the sun sets.

☎ 9365 6044 🖳 trio _bondi@yahoo.com.au ✉ **56 Campbell Pde, Bondi** 🕑 **6-10pm Mon & Tue, 8.30am-4pm & 6pm-late Wed-Sun**

CHINATOWN & DARLING HARBOUR

To get to Chinatown, take the train to Central, the Monorail to Power-house Museum, the MLR to Haymarket or the ferry to Darling Harbour and stroll south a short way. Darling Park Monorail and Convention MLR stops are closer to the Darling Harbour foody action.

BBQ King (5, C8) $$
Cantonese
Low on ambience but big on flavour, the King serves up royal portions of roast duck, suckling pig and other Cantonese staples. You might need a Tsing Tao or three to stay sane amid the mildly obnoxious chaos. Take away bald glazed ducks next door. Open late.
☎ 9267 2433 ✉ 18-20 Goulburn St, Chinatown
🕑 11.30am-2am ♿ Ⓥ

Blackbird (5, C7) $$
Mod Oz Café
This place veritably thrums from the minute it opens its doors for breakfast. Funky young staff cruise the cool décor delivering hearty bowls of pasta, pizzas from the hot-stone oven and fat triangles of cake. Perfect to fuel up before or after a big night out.
☎ 9283 7385 🖥 www .blackbirdcafe.com.au
✉ Balcony, Cockle Bay Wharf, Darling Harbour
🕑 8am-late ♿ fair
♿ Ⓥ

Bungalow 8 (5, B5) $$
Seafood
Retreat to the far end of King St Wharf if the

Chinta Ria – roll up to the Temple of Love

mayhem of Darling Harbour starts to melt your mind. Slink into a low leather booth on the cool slate floor, watch the harbour lights and slurp a lemon-grass laksa stacked high with fresh mussels. The Loft Bar upstairs has cocktails afterwards.
☎ 9299 4660 🖥 www .bungalow8sydney.com
✉ 8 The Promenade, King St Wharf, Darling Harbour
🕑 noon-late ♿ good

Cargo Bar (5, B6) $$
Mod Oz
The definitive Darling Harbour bar also has a well defined kitchen. Beautiful boys, babes and backpack-ers get wall-to-wall boozy after 11pm – before they descend, sit back, drink in

the harbour views and enjoy fine pizzas and salads. DJs fire it up most nights; jazz mellows it down on Sunday afternoons.
☎ 9262 1777 🖥 www .cargobar.com.au ✉ 52 The Promenade, King St Wharf, Darling Harbour
🕑 11am-late ♿ good

Chinta Ria, Temple of Love (5, C7) $$
Malaysian
Swirling choreographically around an enormous con-crete Buddha, Chinta Ria's temple-in-the-round setting serves up zingy Malaysian hawker-style food at reason-able prices. Go with a rabble of friends and share plates of Hokkien noodles, sambal prawns, seafood laksa, superbly slippery fried *kuay teow* and flaky roti bread.
☎ 9264 3211; fax 9264 1411 ✉ Roof Terrace, L2 Cockle Bay Wharf, Darling Harbour
🕑 noon-2.30pm, 6-11pm ♿ fair ♿ Ⓥ

Tipping
A 10% tip is customary for good restaurant service, but feel free to vary the amount depending on your satisfaction reaction.

Concrete (5, C7) $$
Mod Oz

OK, so it's not technically *in* Darling Harbour, but Concrete is handy for a bite if you're mooching around Pyrmont or the Sydney Fish Markets. True to form, there's a lot of minimalist concrete going on here, but plenty of noise and laughter, too. Try the chubby prawn linguini.
☎ 9518 9523
🖳 concrete8@bigpond.com.au ✉ 224 Harris St, Pyrmont 🕑 7am-4pm Mon-Fri, 8am-4pm Sat & Sun Ⓥ options

Golden Century (5, C9) $$$
Cantonese Seafood

This bustling restaurant cooks up crustaceans straight from the tank that forms a window-wall to the street. That's a whole lot o' nervously squabbling coral trout, king crab, barramundi, lobster and abalone. Splash out on the whole lobster cooked in ginger and shallots: tank–net–kitchen–you.
☎ 9212 3901 🖳 www.goldencentury.com.au ✉ 393-9 Sussex St, Chinatown 🕑 noon-4am 🖐

Xic Lo (5, C9) $$
Vietnamese

Xic Lo's shiny, angled, stainless-steel interior is a glossy departure from the *pho* houses of yore. The menu though is reassuringly familiar: fresh rice paper rolls, vermicelli salads, piping-hot bowls of aromatic *pho* soup (slippery

Duck! BBQ King

rice noodles, fragrant basil and beef) are the stars.
☎ 9280 1678 ✉ 215a Thomas St, Chinatown (entry from Ultimo Rd) 🕑 11am-10.30pm, to 10pm Sun 🖐 fair 🖐 Ⓥ

CITY CENTRE

Aqua Luna (5, E3) $$$
Italian

Check out some surf videos over a pre-dinner drink at the underwater-vibe bar downstairs, then head upstairs for tastes turned up to the max. Thick Jerusalem artichoke soup is laced with pungent olive oil; the veal-and-thyme lasagne is a marriage made in heaven.
☎ 9251 0311 🖳 www.aqualuna.com.au ✉ Shop 8, Opera Quays, Circular Quay East 🕑 noon-3pm Mon-Fri, 5.30-11pm Mon-Sun 🚉 🚌 🚢 Circular Quay 🖐 fair Ⓥ options

Aria (5, E3) $$$$
Modern European

Aria is a star in Sydney's fine-dining firmament, an award-winning combination of masterful dishes, awesome views of the Harbour Bridge and Opera House (*is* there a more beautiful building?) and faultless service. The seared tuna nicoise and mouth-watering lamb rack will have you on the verge of tears.
☎ 9252 2555 🖳 www.ariarestaurant.com.au ✉ 1 Macquarie St 🕑 noon-3pm & 5.30-11pm Mon-Fri, 5.30-11pm Sat, 6-10pm Sun 🚉 🚌 🚢 Circular Quay 🖐 fair

Bodhi (5, E7) $$
Chinese/Vegan

Bodhi scores high for its cool design and leafy position. Quick-fire waiters bounce off stainless-steel minimalism inside and slatted wooden tables and umbrellas outside. Have a swim at the pool before daily yum cha, a relaxed and value-for-money affair. The barbeque buns rock.
☎ 9360 2523 ✉ Cook & Phillip Park, Cathedral St, East Sydney 🕑 10am-11pm, to 4pm Mon, yum cha 10am-5pm 🚉 Museum, St James 🖐 good 🖐 Ⓥ

Cadmus (5, E3) $$$$
Eastern Mediterranean

Cadmus is a dream of spectacular visions: sexy receptionists greet you and lead you to your table, exterior views stretch from the Heads to the Bridge, original Chagall and Picasso

Business Eats

Business in Sydney can be frantic, but everyone's got to eat sometime. **Aria** (p67), **Forty One** (p69), **Pier** (p78) and **Prime** (p69) provide a private, calm and comfortable atmosphere where you can meet clients, chew the fat and close the deal.

paintings line the walls as art-designed platefuls of Middle Eastern inspired food arrive. Don't dream it's over, there's still dessert...
☎ 9252 6800 🖳 www.cadmus.com.au ✉ L10, 3 Macquarie St, Circular Quay East 🕒 noon-3pm & 6-11pm 🚉 🚌 🛳 Circular Quay 🚻 good 🅥 options

Cafe Sydney (5, D4) $$$
Mod Oz
A capacious dining hall on the Customs House roof with outrageous harbour views, outdoor terrace, glass ceiling, cocktail bar, live Friday-night jazz and gun chef Stewart Wallace; the list of Cafe Sydney's pluses is as long as your arm. Seafood and wok dishes rule the roost.
☎ 9251 8683 🖳 www.cafesydney.com ✉ L5,

Aqua Luna – wonderful

Customs House, Circular Quay 🕒 noon-11pm 🚉 🚌 🛳 Circular Quay 🚻 fair 🅥 options

Civic Dining (5, D8) $$
Mod Oz
The dining areas in this Art Deco pub have an understated elegance. The weekend drag queens downstairs do not. Whichever you prefer, the internationally inspired menu and wine/cocktail lists are superb (try a pussy-whipped appassionata). The warm Asian-duck salad, deco pizzas and sticky fig pudding take the cake.
☎ 8080 7040 🖳 www.civichotel.com.au ✉ cnr Pitt & Goulburn Sts 🕒 noon-3pm Tue-Fri, 6-10.30pm Tue-Sat, supper 10pm-late Fri & Sat 🚉 Museum Ⓜ World Square

Edna's Table (5, C6) $$$
Native Australian
Sydney's leading exponent of 'bush tucker', Edna's sits on a staid section of Clarence St pursuing a risqué combination of native ingredients and European techniques. The results, like the gumleaf-smoked grilled salmon and wattleseed pavlova, are triumphant.
☎ 9267 3933 🖳 www.ednastable.com.au ✉ 204 Clarence St

🕒 noon-2.30pm Mon-Fri, 6-9.30pm Tue-Sat 🚉 Town Hall Ⓜ Galleries Victoria

Est. (5, D4) $$$$
Modern European
Pressed-tin ceilings, huge columns, oversize windows and modern furniture make Est. a must-see for the décor as much as the food. Menu stunners include slow-roasted quail on perfectly textured, white-asparagus risotto, and baked baby barramundi. Zealous wine attendants will fetch your desired champagne from the superb cellar.
☎ 9240 3031 🖳 www.merivale.com ✉ L1, Establishment Hotel, 252 George St 🕒 noon-2.30pm & 6-11pm Mon-Fri, 6-11pm Sat 🚉 Circular Quay, Wynyard 🚌 🛳 Circular Quay 🚻 good

Guillaume at Bennelong (5, E3) $$$$
Mod Oz
Turn the old 'dinner and a show' cliché into something meaningful at the Sydney Opera House. Snuggle into a banquette and enjoy acclaimed chef Guillaume Brahimi's masterful cuisine. His basil-infused tuna with mustard seed and soy vin-aigrette has fans hollering operatically all over town.
☎ 9241 1999 🖳 www.guillaumeatbennelong.com.au ✉ Sydney Opera House 🕒 5.30-11pm Mon-Wed & Sat, noon-3pm & 5.30-late Thu & Fri, 6-10pm Sun 🚉 🚌 🛳 Circular Quay 🚻 fair 🅥 options

Prime (5, D5) $$$
Steak House

Need a large dose of iron? Venture into this carnivores' paradise, deep in a dark, subterranean sandstone bunker. The succulent 400g, aged rib-eye with silky potato mash and a red wine sauce is a protein-packed knock out. Digest over a drink next door at **Senate** (☎ 9229 7766) afterwards. ☎ 9229 7777 ▯ www .gposydney.com ✉ LG, GPO Bldg, 1 Martin Pl 🕙 noon-3pm Mon-Fri, 6-10pm Mon-Sat 🚇 Martin Place Ⓥ (nah, just kidding)

Quadrant (5, E4) $$$
Mod Oz

Quadrant does nothing by quarters. It offers the whole dining experience (perhaps 'Circle' is a more fitting name?). Floor-to-ceiling windows with amazing views, exceptional service (maître d', Bernard, is a classic) and thrilling dishes, like barramundi with salmon and

No-one cuts corners at Quadrant

Vietnamese salad, make for a well-rounded experience. ☎ 9256 4000; fax 9265 4040 ✉ L2, Quay Grand Suites, 61 Macquarie St, Circular Quay East 🕙 7-10am, noon-2.30pm & 7-9pm Mon-Fri, 5.30-10pm Sat 🚇 🚌 🚢 Circular Quay ♿ good Ⓥ options

Tetsuya's (5, C7) $$$$
French/Japanese

Down a clandestine security driveway, Tetsuya's could

well be the ultimate dining experience. Japanese-born Tetsuya Wakuda creates morsels of fusion food with megabytes of flavour. You'll find a perfect match for the confit of ocean trout with roe in the 3000-bottle wine cellar. Book way ahead. ☎ 9267 2900; fax 9262 7099 ✉ 529 Kent St 🕙 noon-1.30pm Fri & Sat, 6.30-9pm Tue-Sat 🚇 Town Hall Ⓜ World Square

---

Gastronomic Panoramics

Sydney's stupendous setting offers some kickin' combinations of vistas and victuals:

Catalina (2, E4; ☎ 9371 0555; www.catalinarosebay.com.au; 1 Sunderland Ave, Rose Bay) Shark Island views in a WWII flying-boat base.

Forty One (5, E5; ☎ 9221 2500; www.forty-one.com.au; L42, Chifley Tower, 2 Chifley Square) Luxury dining; harbour sights and lights.

Nielsen Park Kiosk (2, E3; ☎ 9337 1574; www.npk.com.au; Greycliffe Ave, Nielsen Park, Vaucluse) Upmarket Italian with beach and harbour outlooks.

Summit (5, D5; ☎ 9247 9777; www.summitrestaurant.com.au; L47, Australia Sq) Revolving vistas, great food and a retro-cool interior.

Unkai (Shangri-La Hotel, 5, C4; ☎ 9250 6123; www.shangri-la.com; L36, 176 Cumberland St, The Rocks) Japanese fine dining with a harbour panorama.

Wharf (5, C2; ☎ 9250 1761; www.thewharfrestaurant.com.au; Pier 4, Hickson Rd, Walsh Bay) Picture-postcard views and magical Mod Oz meals.

DARLINGHURST

To get to Victoria St, Liverpool St and Darlinghurst Rd, take a train to Kings Cross, or bus 330, 323-7, 365, 366, 387, 389 or L24.

bills (6, C3) $$
Mod Oz
Sydney loves Bill Granger's restaurant with its sun-filled room and huge communal table. Breakfast dishes like ricotta hotcakes with fruit and honeycomb butter, and sweetcorn fritters with roast tomato, spinach and bacon are worth writing home about. **bills 2** (6, A5; ☎ 9360 4762; 359 Crown St, Surry Hills) opens for dinner. ☎ 9380 5420 ⌨ bills @billsfood.com ✉ 433 Liverpool St ⏰ 7.30am-3pm Mon-Sat, 8.30am-3pm Sun ♿ Ⓥ options

Fu Manchu (6, C3) $$
Asian
This hectic, modern noodle bar (Hong Kong chic with communal table and pots of red chopsticks) is as small as a stamp. Slide in sideways for a seat and try the chicken laksa, chilli-salt tempura prawns or vegie buns. Grab a bottle of fish sauce or some dried mushrooms on the way out. ☎ 9360 9424 ⌨ www .fumanchu.com.au ✉ 249 Victoria St ⏰ 5.30-10.30pm Tue-Sun ♿ fair Ⓥ

Oh! Calcutta! (6, C3) $$$
Modern Indian
Oh! Goat curry! This place dishes up north Indian cuisine with a twist in a contemporary setting. Jazz plays as patrons tuck into tandoori quail or duck curry with kipfler potatoes and leeks and desserts like *rasmalai* (rosewater and cardamom–flavoured ricotta dumplings). ☎ 9360 3650 ⌨ www .ohcalcutta.com.au ✉ 251 Victoria St ⏰ 6-10.30pm Mon-Sat Ⓥ options

Onde (6, C3) $$
French
Culturally enriching, palate-pleasing and great value – no wonder Onde is always packed. Some Darlinghursters eat here three times a week for the great service, adventurous wine list and trad faves like pork and duck terrine, lamb tenderloin and buttermilk pudding with berries. ☎ 9331 8749; fax 9331 8759 ✉ 446 Liverpool St ⏰ 5.30am-11pm, to 11.30pm Fri & Sat, to 10pm Sun

Salt (6, B3) $$$$
Mod Oz
Gourmet pleasure seekers and the celebrity A-list haggle for space at this world-class mauve and chrome–toned restaurant. Chef Luke Mangan creates ingenious harmonies and combinations; a pan-fried snapper fillet with roasted zucchini, garlic puree, thyme, grapes and grappa is as tasty and photogenic as the clientele. ☎ 9332 2566 ⌨ www .saltrestaurant.com.au ✉ Kirketon Hotel, 229 Darlinghurst Rd ⏰ 6-11pm Thu-Sat Ⓥ options

---

Hip Herbivores

Enter the realm of tofu, tempeh, soy and greens:

Bodhi (p67)

Govinda's Cinema & Restaurant (6, B3; ☎ 9380 5155; www.govindas.com.au; 112 Darlinghurst Rd) Indian vego smorgasbord and movies on cushions.

Green Gourmet (2, B5; ☎ 9519 5330; www.greengourmet.com.au; 115 King St, Newtown) Serenity and comfort food; serve yourself and pay per kilo.

Iku Wholefood (2, B5; ☎ 9692 8720; fax 9692 8720; 25a Glebe Point Rd) One of several Ikus; munch macro burgers or tofu fritters in the sunken courtyard.

Macro (p57)

mofo (2, B4; ☎ 9555 5811; mofocat@aol.com; 354 Darling St, Balmain) Bohemian and chilled; try a stack of corn fritters with 'mofo chai'.

Mother Chu's Vegetarian Kitchen (5, D8; ☎ 9283 2828; 367 Pitt St) Asian ingredients blended into vego delights beneath the Sydney Monorail.

INNER WEST

From Circular Quay take buses 431-4, 441-2, 445-6 to Balmain; 431-4 to Glebe; 370, 413, 436-40 or 446 to Leichhardt; and 355, 370, 422-3, 426 or 428 to Newtown, which also has a train station.

Balmain

Balmain Eating House (2, B4) $$
French/Mod Oz

The menu here emphasises *enjoying* your food. Hearty breakfast helpings of scrambled eggs, or a shared dessert of pavlova with passionfruit coulis, charm all and sundry. Line up for weekend breakfast at beaten-up tables under hanging garlic wreaths and erotic nymph paintings. Book for dinner.
☎ 9810 3415 ✉ 359 Darling St ☾ 9am-3pm & 6.30pm-late Mon-Sat, from 8am Sat, 8am-3pm Sun

Canteen (2, B4) $
Café

Quick service, great BLTs on French bread (baked on the premises), an 'eggs any way' combo and big cakes – not quite the tray-and-slops mess hall the name suggests. With large communal and pavement tables, eat *en famille* and let the bairns hassle rich ladies' dogs.
☎ 9818 1521 ✉ 332 Darling St ☾ 7am-10pm Mon-Sat, 8am-10pm Sun ♿ footpath only ⚥

Welcome Hotel (2, B4) $$$
Mod Oz

If you get lost in the backstreets of Balmain, you might find yourself chowing down at the Welcome Hotel's dining room. A winter's day calls for the beef and Murphy's pie or veal tenderloin wrapped in pros-

Mind your manors: Badde Manors, Glebe

ciutto. In summer, make for the palm-shaded courtyard, order an unwooded chardonnay and think seafood.
☎ 9810 1323 ▢ www .thewelcomehotel.com ✉ 91 Evans St ☾ 11am-midnight Mon-Sat, noon-10pm Sun ♿ fair

Glebe

Badde Manors (2, A5) $
Café

The feeling's eclectically old-world, but Badde Manors is a new-age kinda joint. It can get hectic here, so don't take offence if the staff are a tad brusque – it's not called Badde Manors for nothing. Dogs sleep blissfully outside, and the cakes and tarts look good enough to eat.
☎ 9660 3797 ✉ 37 Glebe Point Rd ☾ 8am-midnight Mon-Thu, to 1am Fri, 9am-midnight Sun ♿ footpath only ⚥ Ⓥ

Spanish Tapas (2, B5) $$
Spanish

This is a good-time restaurant: waiters who say, 'Yezz, we jave a table forl yo', low

lights, shared tapas plates, spirited music and raucous diners. A jug of sangria will dissolve any resistance to the party vibe and get you stoked for flamenco dancing displays.
☎ 9571 9005; fax 9518 6371 ✉ 28 Glebe Point Rd ☾ 6-11pm ⚥ Ⓥ

Thai On Wok (2, B4) $
Thai

Huh? Sydney's got hundreds of cheap Thai takeaways, what's so good about the this one? The food, my friends, the food. Huddle around laminated tables with students, suits and off-duty cops for bowls of thick noodle soup, sticky satays and chilli-cashew stir-fries, the best this side of Bangers.
☎ 9660 9011 ✉ 193 Glebe Point Rd ☾ 11am-11pm Ⓥ

Leichhardt

Barzu (2, A5) $$
Italian

Book a window table at Barzu – make your selection from the confident wine list, treat yourself to some fine pasta, veal or gourmet pizza, listen to Ronnie tinkling the ivories over terrazzo tiles and watch the Lamborghinis and Alfas cruise Norton St. If the window's taken, the mezzanine awaits...

☎ 9550 0144 🖳 www .barzu.com.au ✉ 121 Norton St ⏰ noon-3.30pm & 5.30-late Mon-Fri, noon-late Sat & Sun

Elio (2, A5) $$$
Italian

Elio's simple, elegant décor and chef Emmanuel Citton's superb risottos and house-made egg pasta transcends the Norton St fray. Risotto not your thing? Try a braised octopus, fennel and orange salad followed by a fresh fruit *crème brûlée*.

☎ 9560 9129 ✉ 159 Norton St ⏰ 6-10.30pm Ⓥ options

Grappa (2, A4) $$$$
Italian

Grappa's open kitchen, snappy bar and elegant dining room with cream-leather seats provide the setting for rich, succulent dishes (braised baby goat on a parmesan risotto) and bounteous wood-fired pizzas. If it's warm, sit outside on the terrace, sip chianti and think of Tuscany. Ahhh, Tuscany...

☎ 9560 6090 🖳 www .grappa.com.au ✉ Shop 1, 267-77 Norton St ⏰ 6-10pm Mon, noon-3pm & 6-10pm Tue-Fri, 6-11pm Sat, 6-9.30pm Sun ♿ good

Newtown
Kilimanjaro (2, B5) $$
African

Kilimanjaro 's cosy tables, carved-wooden bowls, saffron aromas and cheery atmosphere will raise your appetite high above the Serengeti. Authentic and fusion dishes, like the Yassa (chicken on the bone marinated in spicy tomato sauce) are generous and filling. And check out the wicked Africa mural on the alleyway wall!

☎ 9557 4565; fax 9565 1869 ✉ 280 King St ⏰ 6-10pm, to 11pm Sat & Sun, 1-3pm Wed-Sun Ⓥ

Old Fish Shop Cafe (2, B5) $
Café

In a converted fish shop (no prizes for figuring that out), this is Newtown's tattooed, dreadlocked, caffeine hub. Friendly pierced staff will fix you a double shot as you put your feet up on the cushions in the window and watch the action on the street.

☎ 9550 6015 ✉ 239a King St ⏰ 6am-7pm, to 8pm summer ♿ Ⓥ

Thai Pothong (2, B5) $$
Thai

This place has won more Thai Association 'Best Thai Restaurant in Sydney' awards than you've had tom yum soups. Oddly romantic, it's a food hall with the usual collection of carvings suspended from the ceiling. Pull up a window seat and watch the Newtown freak show pass onwards to oblivion.

☎ 9550 6277 🖳 www .thaipothong.com.au ✉ 294 King St ⏰ noon-3pm Tue-Sun, 6-10pm daily, to 11pm Fri & Sat ♿ Ⓥ

Hook, Line & Beer Batter

Sydney serves up a giant platter of marinated, grilled, baked and steamed seafood restaurant options. Here are five of the best:

Boathouse on Blackwattle Bay (2, B4; ☎ 9518 9011; www.bluewaterboat house.com.au; end of Ferry Rd, Glebe) Western harbour views and bold kitchen offerings, including an exquisite snapper pie.

Fishface (6, B3; ☎ 9332 4803; fax 9332 2971; 132 Darlinghurst Rd) Small, busy space serving innovative seafood. Try the blue-eye on potato scales with a salt, pepper and lemon crust.

Mohr Fish (6, A5; ☎ 9318 1326; 202 Devonshire St, East Sydney) Just like an East End London eel-and-mash shop innit geeza, except for the prawn-and-fish dumplings with chilli salsa.

Manta Ray (6, B1; ☎ 9332 3822; fax 9332 3655; 7 The Wharf, Cowper Wharf Rd, Woolloomooloo) Chilled Chardonnay and Manta Ray's fish of the day.

Watermark (p78)

POTTS POINT & WOOLLOOMOOLOO

To get to Potts Point, take a train to Kings Cross, or catch bus 330, 323-7, 365, 366, 387 or L24. Bus 311 runs to Woolloomooloo from Circular Quay.

Fratelli Paradiso (6, C1) $$
Italian

This stylish bistro-bakery has them queuing at the door. The intimate, mod room showcases seasonal Italian dishes cooked with Mediterranean zing. The Rolling Stones lips–inspired wallpaper provides an appropriately salivary backdrop for the signature Calamari Sant'Andrea.
☎ 9357 1744 ✉ 12-16 Challis Ave, Potts Point ☽ 7am-11pm Mon-Fri, to 5pm Sat & Sun ♿ good Ⓥ options

Harry's Cafe de Wheels (6, B1) $
Takeaway Café

For over 50 years, cab drivers, sailors and boozed-up nocturnals have slurred orders for pea-and-pie floaters at Harry's famous counter. Sit on a milk crate overlooking hulking warships and gulp down a 'tiger' (pie, peas, mashed potatoes and gravy). Deadly.
☎ 9357 3074 ✉ www .harryscafedewheels.com .au ✉ Cowper Wharf Rd, Woolloomooloo ☽ 7.30am-1am Sun-Thu, 9am-4am Fri & Sat ♿ ⚇

Kingsleys Steak & Crab-house (6, B1) $$$
Surf 'n' Turf

With its own private marina, your only option is to sail the morning away, moor out the front, uncork a

Fratelli Paradiso: paradisical pastries

bottle of Verdelho and order plates of salt and pepper–crusted or Singapore chilli crab. As the sun-low sky deepens to orange, Woolloomooloo Bay just might be heaven.
☎ 9331 7788 ✉ www .steak.com.au ✉ 10 The Wharf, Cowper Wharf Rd, Woolloomooloo ☽ noon-10pm Mon-Fri, to 10.30pm Sat, to 9pm Sun ♿ good ⚇ Ⓥ options

Matchbox (6, C2) $
Café

It's probably directly linked to endless nights of party-love, but big breakfasts are something Sydney does well. Matchbox, only a bit bigger than its namesake, does one of the best. Locals, backpackers, style queens and film makers squish in for scrambled eggs with field mushrooms and asparagus, or Adam's chicken schnitzel sandwiches.
☎ 9326 9860 ✉ 197 Victoria St, Potts Point

☽ 7am-5pm Mon-Sat, 8am-5pm Sun ⚇ Ⓥ options

Nove (6, B1) $$
Italian

Pizza by the slice ain't ever tasted quite this good. A million miles from your suburban pizza shop, Nove, with boardwalk water views and Philippe Starck furniture, is packed with celebs and after-movie crowds. Try the prosciutto, tomato, goats-cheese and rocket pizza for a gutsy kick in the pants.
☎ 9368 7599; fax 9360 9688 ✉ 9 The Wharf, Cowper Wharf Rd, Woolloomooloo ☽ noon-11pm, to 9pm Sun ♿ good Ⓥ options

Otto (6, B1) $$$$
Italian

Otto's Melburnian chef Maurizio Tersini has revolutionised Italian cooking in Sydney. Forget the glamorous waterfront location and A-list crowd; the food

Breakfast? Just think 'Zinc'

is the business. Dishes like *strozzapreti con gamberi* (artisan pasta with fresh Yamba prawns, tomato, chilli and black olives) define culinary perfection.

Don't entertain thoughts of not booking.
☎ 9368 7488 ▢ www .otto.net.au ✉ 8 The Wharf, Cowper Wharf Rd, Woolloomooloo ◷ noon-midnight ♿ good Ⓥ options

Shimbashi Soba (6, B1) $$
Japanese
Harmonious interior shades of jade, charcoal and dark wood are enhanced by the lapping waters just beyond the boardwalk. Order the salty soba chips, chilled tofu or a bowl of tempura udon – deliciously chunky noodles swimming in a savoury broth with lightly fried fish and vegies.
☎ 9357 7763; fax 9357 7675 ✉ 6 The Wharf, Cowper Wharf Rd, Woolloomooloo ◷ noon-2.30pm & 6-10pm ♿ good Ⓥ

Zinc (6, C1) $$
Café
Surviving the tangible Kings Cross/Potts Point post-Olympic depression, Zinc continues to serve bold breakfasts. There's minimal decoration, lots of glass and too many hard decisions to make at 8am. The pancakes with spiced plum sauce, or eggs with sugar-cured salmon? Bring a mate and order both.
☎ 9358 6777 ▢ zincbar@ihug.com.au ✉ 77 Macleay St, Potts Point ◷ 7am-7pm ♿ outside only Ⓥ options

SURRY HILLS

To get to Surry Hills, catch the train or MLR to Central Station – it's a hop, skip and a jump east from here.

Billy Kwong (6, A4) $$
Chinese
Chef Kylie Kwong's novel take on Chinese cuisine soon explains why this hip eating house is always so busy. You can't go wrong with a staple like spicy, diced, fried green beans with hoisin and garlic, or a generous serve of Kylie's signature dish, the crispy-skin duck with plum sauce.
☎ 9332 3300; fax 9332 4109 ✉ 3-355 Crown St ◷ 6-10pm Mon-Sat, to 9pm Sun ♿ fair Ⓥ

Cafe Niki (6, A6) $
Café
Lovers converge in battered-leather nooks, broadsheet newspaper readers battle

the breeze on streetside stools, daydreamers occupy window seats, whisperers lean intently towards one other at tiny marble-topped tables and loners ponder life in the courtyard. Coffee and café fare; come as you are…
☎ 9319 7517 ✉ 544 Bourke St ◷ 7am-10pm Mon-Fri, 8am-10pm Sat, 8am-4pm Sun ♿ Ⓥ

Clove (6, A4) $$
Indian
Owner Nash has been cooking up a mean mountain of curry here for 12 years, filling the tables without so much as a hint of advertising. Word of mouth is a powerful force, almost as powerful as

Nash's special lamb shank and chicken curries.
☎ 9361 0980; fax 9361 0987 ✉ 249 Crown St ◷ 11.30am-3pm Mon-Fri (bookings only), 5.30-11pm, to 11.30pm Fri & Sat ♿ Ⓥ

Dragonfly (6, A5) $$
Asian
This sexy, self-described 'sushi deli noodle bar' pays attention to detail, successfully melding Japanese dishes with pan-Asian flair. Order beautifully proportioned sashimi and sushi, or try the steamed wild barramundi perfectly pitched with ginger garlic soy, Chinese cabbage and enoki mushrooms.

☎ 9380 7333 ✉ 478
Bourke St ⏰ 6-10pm
Tue-Sat Ⓥ

Fringe Cafe (5, D9) $$
Organic Café

The owners of the nightclub
that used to be here left
town in a hurry, making
way for Sydney's first fully
licensed, certified organic
restaurant. Proprietor
Betty Leone's magnificent
lasagnes and frittatas are
the chosen fare of architects
and business bods on
lunchtime city sabbatical.
☎ 9280 1161
💻 betty@fringecafe
.com.au ✉ 23-33 Mary St
⏰ 8am-5.30pm Mon-Fri,
9am-3pm Sat ♿ good
Ⓥ vegetarian & vegan

Longrain (5, D8) $$$
Thai

Longrain makes serving
dozens of famished, fussy
diners looks easy. Inside a
century-old, wedge-shaped
printing-press building, ur-
banites snack on chef Martin
Boetz's delicacies like red
beef and snakebean curry or
braised beef shin with mint,
coriander and red chilli. Sip
caipiroskas at the adjacent
bar until the wee smalls.
☎ 9280 2888 💻 www.lo
ngrain.com.au ✉ 85 Com-

> ### Table for One, Please...
>
> Eating alone should be an indulgence, your full at-
> tentions given to the food and the dining experience
> (or maybe a book). But too often restaurants adopt
> a 'What's wrong pal, got no friends?' attitude. Here
> are some places soloists will feel at home:
>
> **bills** (p70) Nab a spot on the communal table near
> the stack of pomegranates for brilliant breakfasts.
>
> **Longrain** (below) High stools at a deep bar for
> Asian curries and Brazilian *caipiroskas* (vodka,
> crushed fresh lime and sugar syrup).
>
> **Sailors Thai Canteen** (p76) The long communal
> table here almost extends to Khao San Rd. Slide in
> and order a spicy beef salad.

monwealth St ⏰ noon-
3pm & 6-11pm Mon-Fri,
6-11pm Sat; bar 5.30pm-
midnight ♿ fair Ⓥ

Marque (6, A5) $$$
Modern French

Marque's elegant interior
resonates perfectly with
sophisticated and adventurous food. Crispy-red mullet
is served with sea urchin
custard, blood sausage and
cuttlefish ink; roast New
England muscovy duck is
smothered with liquorice
nicoise olive emulsion and
lemon confit.
☎ 9332 2225 💻 www
.marquerestaurant.com
✉ 355 Crown St ⏰ 6.30-
10pm Mon-Sat ♿ fair

MG Garage (6, A5) $$$$
Mod Oz

Contemporary cuisine in elegant automotive surrounds.
The seasonal menu has an
individual take on Australian produce with dishes
like cured ocean trout with
crayfish, or fillet of snapper
with salt-cod purée. Peugeot
or Volvo more your style?
Steer into the **Fuel Bistro**
(☎ 9383 9388) next door.
☎ 9360 7007 💻 www
.mggaragesydney.com.au
✉ 490 Crown St ⏰ noon-
2.30 Tue-Fri, 6.30pm-late
Tue-Sat Ⓥ options

Tabou (6, A6) $$$
French

Not out of place on Boulevard
Saint-Michel, the décor and
lilting accordion music are
French to the core. Brasserie
food, including perennial
faves like duck confit, *lapin
de la moutard* and steak tar-
tare, paints the scene Gallic.
Buvez et mangez, c'est bon!
☎ 9319 5682 💻 www
.tabourestaurant.com
.au ✉ 527 Crown St
⏰ 6.30pm-late daily,
noon-2.30 Mon-Fri

THE ROCKS

To get to The Rocks, take the train, bus or ferry to Circular Quay and head west.

Bel Mondo (5, D3) $$$$
Italian
In Sydney's culinary hall of fame, chef Neil Pass has serious cred. Expect northern Italian cuisine perfectly executed in dramatic surrounds – space, elegance and pizzazz; *very* Sydney. For a more relaxed meal, their cool and casual **Antibar** is perfect for an quick lunch, after-work cocktail or late-night supper.
☎ 9241 3700 ▢ www .belmondo.com.au ✉ L3, Argyle Stores, Gloucester Walk, The Rocks ◔ noon-2.30pm Tue-Fri, 6.30-10.30pm Mon-Thu, to 11pm Fri, Sat & Sun

Cruise (5, D3) $$$
Mod Oz
Posh cocktail lounge upstairs wallows in lugubrious style. **Cruise Bar** downstairs does a roaring trade every night. In between, Cruise restaurant cooks up satisfying serves of prawn-and-scallop dumplings with red vinegar and local snapper fillet with shaved fennel, prawns and tomato vinaigrette. Tasty work.
☎ 9251 1188 ▢ www .cruisebar.tv ✉ Overseas Passenger Terminal, Circular Quay West ◔ noon-2.30pm & 6-10.30pm ◔ good Ⓥ options

Firefly (5, C2) $$
Café/Wine Bar
Compact, classy and never snooty, Firefly's outdoor candlelit tables fill with pre-theatre patrons having a quick meal before the show. Come after 8pm when the audience has taken its seats – savour some fine wine as the scent of money floats over the powerboats in Walsh Bay.
☎ 9241 2031 ▢ www .fireflybar.net ✉ Lot 5, Pier 7, 17 Hickson Rd, Walsh Bay ◔ 7am-10pm Sun-Wed, to 11pm Thu-Sat

harbour kitchen & bar (5, D2) $$$$
Mod Oz
This low-slung wing of the Park Hyatt offers light meals in the bar (amazing club sandwiches and king prawn linguini), while the giant open kitchen cooks up restaurant wonders like twice-cooked duck breast with sherry roasted peaches, spinach and fried leeks. You want Opera House views with that?
☎ 9256 1661 ▢ www .sydney.hyatt.com ✉ Park Hyatt Hotel, 7 Hickson Rd ◔ 6.30-10.30am, noon-2.30pm & 6-10.30pm ◔ good Ⓥ options

Quay (5, D3) $$$
Mod Oz
With all of Sydney's icons on display at once, sitting on the balcony next to the teary, streamer-hurling non-embarkers at the OSPT is surreal. Equally euphoric is the stylish service, outstanding wine list and adventurous cooking (try the pork neck with rare-breed prosciutto, shitake mushrooms and red rice).
☎ 9251 5600 ▢ www .quay.com.au ✉ Overseas Passenger Terminal, Circular Quay West ◔ noon-2.30pm Tue-Fri, 6-10pm daily ◔ good Ⓥ options

Rockpool (5, D3) $$$$
Mod Oz
Behind an unassuming green façade, the Rockpool is arguably Sydney's best restaurant (oh, how they argue), chef Neil Perry's modern seafood creations continuing to wow the critics. Expect crafty, contemporary cuisine with Asian influences, faultless service and an alluring wine list. Perry's signature stir-fried mud crab omelette is a winner.
☎ 9252 1888 ▢ www .rockpool.com ✉ 107 George St ◔ 6-11pm Tue-Sat

Sailors Thai Canteen (5, D3) $$
Thai
Pour yourself into a gap between arts-community operators, politicians and media manoeuvrers at Sailors' long, zinc communal table and order the *som dam* (green papaya, peanut and dried prawn salad). The tables on the balcony fill up fast, but fortune might be smiling on you.
☎ 9251 2466; fax 9251 2610 ✉ 106 George St ◔ noon-10pm Mon-Sat ⏇ Ⓥ

WOOLLAHRA & PADDINGTON

To get to Paddington and Woollahra, catch bus 378, 380, 382 or L82 along Oxford St or 389 through Five Ways and the back streets.

Arthur's Pizza (6, D5) $$
Italian
'Hey Arthur, how come your sign's upside down?' A common question, but it's best not to ask. Instead, cram inside the dark-wood pan-elled dining room and munch a 'Sasha' pizza (marinated lamb, sweet potato, feta and red onion) – it'll go down in history as one of the best. ☎ 9331 1779 ✉ 260 Oxford St ⏱ 5pm-mid-night Mon-Fri, noon-mid-night Sat & Sun Ⓖ Ⓥ

Bistro Lulu (6, D5) $$$
French
Everything here is easy going; the ambience is all embrac-ing, the service polished and the food superior. Try flavour-packed trad champs like duck confit or sirloin steak with *frittes* as the staff fold-back the windows and let the Oxford St atmospheria float in on the tide. ☎ 9380 6888 🖥 www .bistrolulu.com.au ✉ 257 Oxford St ⏱ noon-3pm Thu-Sat, 6pm-late daily Ⓥ options

Bistro Moncur (6, E5) $$$
French
Mini-moguls and luncheon ladies while away long after-noons below vaulted ceilings and Matisse-esque murals out the back of the Wool-lahra Hotel. Dishes like the blue swimmer crab omelette have become ingrained in Sydney's culinary lexicon. The wine list will make you want to take up mogulling too.

☎ 9363 2519 🖥 www .bistromoncur.com.au ✉ 116 Queen St ⏱ noon-3pm Thu-Sun, 6-10.30pm daily, to 9pm Sun

Buon Ricordo (6, C4) $$$$
Italian
Remember the old days, when local restaurateurs knew you well enough to select your meal for you? Well, Buon Ricordo is very 'old days'. Let chef Armando Percuoco decide whether you want the *zuppa di pesce* or the *barciolette reginaldo*. Hmm, best Italian in Sydney, Buon Ricordo or Otto? ☎ 9360 6729 🖥 www .buonricordo.com.au ✉ 108 Boundary St ⏱ noon-2.30pm Fri & Sat, 6.30-10.30pm Tue-Sat (supper 'til midnight)

Buzo (6, E5) $$
Italian
Red-checked tablecloths, subdued lighting and unassuming staff are un-Woollahra in the best

possible way. Heavenly highlights include grilled calamari stuffed with basil and parmesan topped with fresh tomatoes, and a rich honey gelati riddled with caramelised walnuts. If it's raining, they might even lend you an umbrella. ☎ 9328 1600 ✉ 152 Jersey Rd ⏱ 6.30-10pm Mon-Sat Ⓖ Ⓥ options

Gusto (6, D4) $
Café/Deli
Five Ways' beacon of activ-ity, Gusto does everything with gusto. Breakfast rolls (egg, ham, tomato and hol-landaise on an onion roll) nourish skinny actresses on the footpath tables, the spinach and onion frittata is supremely confident while the deli doles out cheeses, pesto, hams and olives with enthused abandon. ☎ 9361 5640; fax 9328 2083 ✉ Five Ways, 2a Heely St ⏱ 7am-8pm Mon-Sat, 7.30am-8pm Sun Ⓚ footpath only Ⓖ Ⓥ

Paddo Pub Grub

Paddington's pubs take the simple concept of a pub counter meal and elevate it to an entirely more sophisticated plane:

Centennial (6, E6; ☎ 9362 3838; www.centennial hotel.com.au; 88 Oxford St, Woollahra)

Grand National (6, E5; ☎ 9363 3096; grand@ alpha.net; 161 Underwood St)

Paddington Inn (6, D5; ☎ 9380 5277; www.pad dingtoninn.com.au; 338 Oxford St)

Royal Hotel (6, D4; ☎ 9331 2604; www.royalhotel .com.au; Five Ways, 237 Glenmore Rd)

WORTH A TRIP

Some salubrious eats on far-flung streets:

**Bathers' Pavilion
(2, D2)** $$$$
Mod Oz
Romantic architecture (1929 Spanish mission–style pavilion), sweeping water views and outstanding food collide to make Bathers' one of Sydney's most popular restaurants. **Bathers' Cafe** offers equally scrumptious fare at more democratic prices.
☎ 9969 5050 🖳 www
.batherspavilion.com.au
✉ 4 The Esplanade, Balmoral 🕒 noon-2.30pm (from 11.30am Sat & Sun) & 6-10.30pm 🚊 Taronga Park Zoo then 🚌 238
♿ good 🚲 🆅 options

**Doyles on the Beach
(2, F3)** $$$
Seafood
King of Sydney seafood for so long, you might think Doyle's are resting on their laurels. Nevertheless, they ain't your average fish-and-chipper, and catching the ferry to Watsons Bay for a seafood lunch with harbour views is a quintessential Sydney experience.
☎ 9337 2007 🖳 www
.doyles.com.au ✉ 11 Marine Pde, Watsons Bay 🚌 324-5, L24, L82 🚊 Watsons Bay 🕒 noon-3pm, 6-9.30pm 🚲 ♿ good

Jonah's (1, E1) $$$$
Mod Oz
Teetering precipitously high above Whale Beach, Jonah's prepares sharp modern dishes (like spicy seafood

sausages) with enough flavour to tear customers away from the bodacious view. Come for dinner, stay the night then rock up for lunch the next day.
☎ 9974 5599 🖳 www
.jonahs.com.au ✉ 69 Bynya Rd, Palm Beach 🕒 noon-2.30pm, 6.30-9.30pm Wed-Sun 🚌 L90 or 190 ♿ good 🆅 options

Le Kiosk (4, C2) $$$
Mod Oz
Le Kiosk defines romance – a sandstone cottage, gentle lighting, open fireplace and the lull of lapping waves. The food proves a worthy paramour; swoon over grilled kingfish and the honeycomb-and-mascarpone parfait with nectarine soup.
☎ 9977 4122 🖳 www
.lekiosk.com.au ✉ 1 Marine Pde, Shelly Beach, Manly 🕒 noon-3pm, to 3.30pm Sun, 6.30-9.30pm Fri, to 10pm Sat, to 9pm Sun 🚊 Manly 🚌 151, 169 or E69 🚲 🆅 options

Pier (2, E4) $$$$
Seafood
Bobbing with the yachts on stilts over Rose Bay, Pier serves exhilarating seafood. Try the seared scallops on kipfer potato confit with baby salad and creamed-truffle vinaigrette, or a meltingly good salmon pastrami. The floorboards are caulked like a yacht – can we set sail with this menu?
☎ 9327 6561; fax 9363 0927 ✉ 594 New

South Head Rd, Rose Bay 🕒 noon-3pm & 6-10pm Mon-Sat, 6-9pm Sun 🚌 323-5 or L24

Watermark (2, E2) $$$
Mod Oz Seafood
This immaculately converted restaurant, once the Balmoral Baths' changing rooms, offers a feast for the eyes and the stomach. The seafood/Asian menu is a perfect match for expansive beach panoramas – relish it over a seafood antipasto. Allow yourself 15min to find a park on weekends.
☎ 9968 3433 🖳 www
.watermarkrestaurant.com
.au ✉ 2a The Esplanade, Balmoral 🕒 7-10.30am, noon-3pm & 6.30-10pm Mon-Fri; 8-10.30am, 12.30-3.30pm & 6.30-10pm Sat & Sun 🚊 Taronga Park Zoo then 🚌 238 ♿ fair

**Woolwich Pier Hotel
(2, B3)** $$
Mod Oz
Trek through the Inner West to the Woolwich peninsula. The pub is pretty much the only building here that isn't a mansion. The balcony is great for an upmarket pub lunch with watery views across Cockatoo Island, Balls Head, Birchgrove and Balmain.
☎ 9817 2204 🖳 www
.woolwichpierhotel.com
.au ✉ 2 Gale St, Woolwich 🕒 noon-3pm & 6-10pm Mon-Fri, noon-4pm & 6-10pm Sat & Sun, to 9pm Sun 🚌 507 to Gladesville then 🚌 359 🚲

Entertainment

Sydney idolises its concert halls and theatres, but loves the beach even more. When accused by other states of anti-intellectualism, Sydneysiders shrug and splash on more sunscreen. Sure, locals have season subscriptions to Opera Australia, the Sydney Theatre Company and the Sydney Symphony, but with so many sunny beaches, it's difficult to focus on earnest indoor pursuits.

After dark, things get busy in venues – from bars and dance clubs to outdoor cinemas, sports stadiums and live-music pubs. Gay and lesbian culture fuels much of the entertainment scene, with nightly drag shows, annual queer film festivals and regular dance parties.

Just the Ticket
Tickets can usually be purchased directly from the venue. Alternatively, **Ticketek** (☎ 9266 4800; www.ticketek.com) and **ticketmaster7** (☎ 136 100; www.ticket master7.com.au) offer credit-card bookings (around $3 booking fee per ticket). The **HalfTix booth** (☎ 9261 2990; www.halftix.com .au), near Darling Park Monorail stop in Darling Harbour, sells unsold tickets at half price on performance day.

Word Up
Pick up the Metro section in Friday's *Sydney Morning Herald* for comprehensive entertainment listings. Free weekly street magazines like *Drum Media*, *3D World* and *Revolver* specialise in gig and club information.

Where It's At
Most of Sydney's entertainment venues are in the following areas:

City Centre, Darling Harbour and The Rocks – concert halls, mainstream theatres, bars and nightclubs

Surry Hills and Redfern – smaller fringe dance and theatre companies

Oxford St, Darlinghurst and King St, Newtown – late-night cafés, gay and lesbian bars and clubs

Newtown, Annandale, Surry Hills and Balmain – live rock, blues and jazz in pubs

Potts Point, Kings Cross and Darlinghurst – nightclubs, hip bars and strip clubs in the Cross

Friday night frenzy on Oxford St

Good Times for Free
Free entertainment proliferates during the summer months with music performances in the parks. January's **Sydney Festival** (p91) offers a plethora of outdoor events; check media for dates. The **Manly International Jazz Festival** in October has free outdoor gigs too.

Weekend **markets** are great places to see street theatre and buskers, as are tourist precincts like Circular Quay, Martin Place Amphitheatre and Darling Harbour. The mad, the erudite and the madly erudite vent their obsessions at **Speakers' Corner** (p36) in The Domain on Sunday afternoons.

There's a free **Aboriginal dance** performance in the Yiribana gallery at the Art Gallery of NSW (p21) at noon Tuesday to Saturday, and the **Tropfest** short-film festival (p87) draws huge crowds to The Domain and various locations on Victoria St, Darlinghurst, on one evening in late February.

SPECIAL EVENTS

January *Sydney Festival* (p91)
Australia Day – 26 January; regatta, tall-ships race, fireworks
Big Day Out – international music mosh at Homebush
Chinese New Year – January/February; Darling Harbour dragon-boat races, food stalls, fireworks, dances, acrobats, buskers, Chinatown parade
Flickerfest – international short-film festival at Bondi Pavilion (☎ 9365 6877; www.flickerfest.com.au)

February *Gay & Lesbian Mardi Gras* (p92)
Tropfest – international short-film festival (p87)

March *Women's Festival* – celebrations coinciding with International Women's Day
Royal Easter Show – March/April; 12 days at Homebush, country animal parade, agricultural flavour, plenty to entertain kids

April *Festival of Fools* – starts 1 April; comedy capers, street performers, outdoor films, Fools Gala at the Town Hall

May *Sydney Writers Festival* – mid- to late May

June *Sydney Film Festival* – mid- to late June; at the State Theatre and Dendy cinemas; whole-season subscriptions or buy tickets to individual screenings (☎ 9280 0511; www.sydneyfilmfestival.org)
Sydney Biennale – held in even years; international arts festival at the Art Gallery of NSW and other city venues

July *Yulefest In the Blue Mountains* – guesthouses and restaurants celebrate Christmas (there might even be snow)

August *Sydney City to Surf* – second Sunday in August; 20,000 runners from Hyde Park to Bondi Beach

September *Royal Botanic Gardens Spring Festival* – early or mid-September; concerts, brass bands, plant market and spring-flower displays in the David Jones city stores
Festival of the Winds – Second Sunday; multicultural kite-flying festival at Bondi Beach
Rugby League Grand Final – at Aussie Stadium (p94)

October *Manly International Jazz Festival* – Labour Day weekend; three days of bebop and za ba de da (☎ 9977 1088)
Sydney Comedy Festival – last three weeks of October; international and local acts, stand-up, theatre and events

November *Sculpture by the Sea* – mid-November; the Bondi to Bronte coastal walk is transformed into a sculpture site

December *Sydney to Hobart Yacht Race* – 26 December; Sydney Harbour is crowded with onlookers for the start of this gruelling race
New Year's Eve – 31 December; fireworks displays over Sydney Harbour

PUBS

Coogee Bay Hotel (2, E6)
This rambling complex has live music at the legendary **Selinas**, a beer garden, open-mic nights, comedy, cocktail lounge, sports bar, bistro and bottle shop. Sit on a stool in the window overlooking the beach, sip a cold one and wait for the perfect set.
☎ 9665 0000 ⌨ www
.coogeebayhotel.com.au
✉ cnr Coogee Bay Rd & Arden St, Coogee 💲 free
🕑 9.30am-3am Thu-Sat, to midnight Sun, to 1am Mon-Wed 🚌 372-4, X73-4, 313-4, 353

Cricketers Arms (6, B5)
This polysexual pub with its crusty, cosy vibe is a favourite haunt of arts students, locals, gays and turntable fans. Ace for a beer anytime, there's also tapas, open fires and the 'Stitch & Bitch' knitting club on Tuesdays.
☎ 9331 3301 ✉ 106 Fitzroy St, Surry Hills 💲 free
🕑 noon-midnight Mon-Sat, noon-10pm Sun
🚆 🚆 Central 🚌 374

Darlo Bar (6, B3) The Darlo's long triangular retro room is a magnet for thirsty urban bohemians with something to read or a hankering for pinball or pool. Afterwards, they roll down the hill to the blue-tiled **Green Park Hotel** (6, C3; ☎ 9380 5311; 360 Victoria St, Darlinghurst).
☎ 9331 3672 ⌨ www
.darlobar.com ✉ Royal Sovereign Hotel, 306 Liverpool St, Darlinghurst
💲 free 🕑 10am-

midnight Mon-Sat, noon-midnight Sun 🚆 Kings Cross 🚌 323-7, 324-5, 333, 389 ♿ fair

Hotel Bondi (3, B1) Let it all hang out at Bondi's landmark 'Pink Palace'. Locals and backpackers play pool, check out bands, ogle big-screen TVs and drink till late. The terrace is good on a sunny day, far away from the poker machines out the back.
☎ 9130 3271 ⌨ www
.hotelbondi.com.au ✉ 178 Campbell Pde, Bondi Beach
💲 free 🕑 10am-4am
🚌 380, 389, L82, 381-2

Lord Nelson Brewery Hotel (5, C3) Built in 1842, the 'Nello' claims to be Sydney's oldest pub (or is it the **Hero of Waterloo** down the road?) The on-site brewery cooks up robust stouts and ales (try the Trafalgar Pale Ale) and there's decent mid-range accommodation upstairs.
☎ 9251 4044 ⌨ www
.lordnelson.com.au ✉ 19 Kent St, Millers Point
💲 free 🕑 11am-11pm

Schooner or middy? See p85...

Mon-Sat, noon-10pm Sun 🚆 🚢 Circular Quay
🚌 339, 431-4

Manly Wharf Hotel (4, A2)
On the harbour side of Manly, the fabulously well-designed Manly Wharf Hotel is perfect for sunny afternoon beers. Have a few middys after a hard day in the surf then pour yourself onto the ferry.
☎ 9977 1266 ⌨ www
.manlywharfhotel.com
.au ✉ Manly Wharf, East Esplanade 💲 free
🕑 11am-midnight Mon-Sat, to 10pm Sun
🚢 Manly Wharf 🚌 151, 169, E69 ♿ excellent

Out On The Tiles
Most of Sydney's older pubs are externally clad in head-high glazed tiles, often with beautifully coloured Art Nouveau designs. Why? Prior to drinking law reform in the mid-'50s, pubs shut their doors at 6pm, before which the after-work crowd would pile in and chug down as many beers as quickly as possible – the **six o'clock swill**. Fast lager plus the sudden requirement of walking caused frequent regurgitations, the nearest wall becoming a prop for the trembling vomiter. Publicans discovered pretty quickly that glazed tiles are easy to hose down.

BARS

Bar Europa (5, D6) Basement vibe, subtle lighting and three debonair rooms divided by sexy screens cement Europa's reputation as an intimate, clubby hideaway for inner-city professionals. Sip a Sydneysider Sour as DJs play laid-back funk, sigh, and wonder what he/she is doing now…
☎ 9232 3377 ▢ info@bareuropa.com.au ✉ Basement, 88 Elizabeth St $ free ☺ 4pm-late Tue-Fri, 8pm-late Sat ▣ Martin Place Ⓜ City Centre

Civic Hotel (5, D8) A chic, three-level Art Deco alcoholiday for continental city slickers. The heritage-tiled street-level saloon gets crowded after work, but it's quieter upstairs on the jazzy terrace or downstairs in the theatre (with live acts like the Church). The restaurant rocks (p68); drag queens overrun the joint on weekends.
☎ 8080 7000 ▢ www.civichotel.com.au ✉ cnr Pitt & Goulburn Sts $ free, live acts vary ☺ 11am-1am Mon-Fri, to 2am Thu, to 4am Fri, 5pm-5am Sat, to midnight Sun ▣ Museum Ⓜ World Square

Establishment (5, D4) Establishment's cashed-up crush proves the art of swilling cocktails after a hard, city day is not lost. Sit at the majestic marble bar, in the swish courtyard or be absorbed by a leather lounge as stockbrokers scribble their phone numbers on the backs of coasters for flirty city girls.
☎ 9240 3000 ▢ www.merivale.com ✉ 252 George St $ free ☺ 11.30am-late Mon-Fri, 6pm-late Sat ▣ Circular Quay, Wynyard 🚌 ⛴ Circular Quay ♿ good

Fix If you're anal about colour coordination, order the raspberry martini. It'll send you into alcoholic raptures and look good next to the red lacquer walls of this boxy bar in the Kirketon Hotel (6, B3), the pinnacle of Sydney style. The less colour-concerned can sniff at the cigar humidor or sip a slow cognac.
☎ 9360 4333 ▢ www.saltrestaurant.com ✉ Kirketon Hotel, 229 Darlinghurst Rd $ free ☺ 6pm-late Tue-Sat ▣ Kings Cross 🚌 330, 323-7, 365, 366, L24

Hemmesphere (5, D4) This private lounge is Sydney's most lustily opulent space; a lush gentlemen-club vibe peppered with Moroccan twists. Sink into a deep, leather chair, order a cigar and mandarin *caipiroska* and wait for Duran Duran to show up. Bookings essential.
☎ 9240 3040 ▢ www.merivale.com ✉ L4, Establishment Hotel, 252 George St $ free ☺ 6pm-2am Tue-Thu, noon-3.30am Fri, 7pm-3.30am Sat ▣ Circular Quay, Wynyard 🚌 ⛴ Circular Quay ♿ good

Hugo's Lounge (6, C3) Sexy surrounds attract a glossy crowd: media celebs

---

Hot Nights, Cool Bars

Questing for the ultimate *caipiroska*? Try these bars with perfect drinks, slick décor and attitudinal splash:

Arthouse Hotel (5, D7; ☎ 9284 1200; www.thearthousehotel.com.au; 275 Pitt St) Three cool bars, Dome restaurant, jazz, dance parties and life drawing will keep you occupied.

Jimmy Liks (6, C2; ☎ 8354 1400; fax 8354 1401; 186 Victoria St, Potts Point) Sophisticated and subtle; Thai-influenced cocktails like the Mekong Mary with chilli *nam jim*.

Mars Lounge (5, E8; ☎ 9267 6440; 16 Wentworth Ave, Surry Hills) Plush red half-moon booths; disco-ball reflections catching your eye – *sooo* money.

Middle Bar (6, B4; ☎ 9331 6200; www.kinselas.com.au; Kinselas, 383-7 Bourke St, Taylor Sq, Darlinghurst) Quaff martinis with Claudia, Cameron and Elle.

Mocean (3, B2; ☎ 9300 9888; mocean@xmsg.com; 34a Campbell Pde, Bondi Beach) Subterranean surfers and their model girlfriends; funk and R&B.

conducting histrionic conversations in between mobile-phone calls. If it feels like a CD launch you weren't invited to, head to the terrace for a stiff drink. Entry ($10) between 7pm and 9pm on Sundays includes cocktails.

☎ 9357 4411 🖳 www .hugos.com.au ✉ L1, 33 Baywater Rd, Kings Cross 💲 free Mon-Thu, $10 Fri, Sat & Sun 🕒 6pm-2am Tue-Thu, noon-3.30am Fri, 7pm-3.30am Sat 🚊 Kings Cross 🚌 330, 323-7, 365, 366, L24

Longrain (5, D9) On balmy summer evenings everyone's dressed in black and wearing those black-rimmed spectacles formerly reserved for physicists: it's Sydney at its most noir. Minimalist décor = plenty of space to sip icy, alcoholic concoctions and spy other suitably louche style-meisters.

☎ 9280 2888 🖳 www .longrain.com.au ✉ 85 Commonwealth St 💲 free 🕒 5.30pm-midnight 🚉 🚌 Central 🚻 fair

Tank Stream Bar (5, D4) After-work suits and stylin' secretaries get high and heady poised over Sydney's original water supply. The Tank Stream runs thick with bottled beer and cocktails, and the corporate mob can't get enough. Neither could Robbie Williams.

☎ 9240 3000 🖳 www .merivale.com ✉ 1 Tank Stream Way 💲 free 🕒 4pm-midnight Mon-Fri, from noon Fri 🚉 Circular Quay, Wynyard 🚌 🚉 Circular Quay 🚻 good

Victoria Room (6, B3) Plush chesterfields, Art Nouveau wallpaper, dark-wood panelling and bamboo screens – the Victoria Room is the spoilt love child of a 1920s Bombay gin palace and a Hong Kong opium den. Don your white linen suit and panama and order a Raspberry Debonair at the bar.

☎ 9357 4488 ✉ L1, 235 Victoria St, Darlinghurst 💲 free 🕒 6pm-midnight Tue-Sat (from 5pm Fri), 4-10pm Sun 🚉 Kings Cross 🚌 330, 323-7, 365, 366, 389, L24

Water Bar (6, B1) Time is meaningless and escape is pointless here (especially after a few martinis). The lofty, romantic space sucks you in to its pink love-world of candles, corners, deep lounges and ottomans as big as king-size beds. Great for business (if you really must), but better for lurve.

☎ 9331 9000 🖳 www .whotels.com ✉ W Sydney Hotel, 6 Cowper Wharf Rd, Woolloomooloo 💲 free 🕒 4pm-midnight, to 10pm Sun & Mon 🚌 311 🚻 good

Civic Hotel: suit up or frock out

ROCK, JAZZ & BLUES

Annandale Hotel (2, B5)
Thankfully, the Annandale escaped the live-music morgue a few years ago and continues to cough up rock, punk and electronica. Inside, Led Zepp wails between sets as afroed punters traverse the sticky carpet. Bands like Jet, the Superjesus, Regurgitator and the Butthole Surfers have played here.
☎ 9550 1078 🖳 www.annandalehotel.com ✉ cnr Parramatta Rd & Nelson St, Annandale 💲 free 🕑 11am-midnight, from noon Sun 🚉 Stanmore 🚌 413, 435-8, 440, 461 ♿ fair

Basement (5, D4)
Sydney's premier jazz venue presents big touring acts (Taj Mahal) and big local talent (Vince Jones). A broad musical mandate also sees funk, blues and soul bands performing plus the odd spoken-word gig. Avoid the standing room—only

bar; book a table close to the stage.
☎ 9251 2797 🖳 www.thebasement.com.au ✉ 29 Reiby Pl, Circular Quay 💲 15+ (varies) 🕑 noon-1.30am Mon-Thu, to 2.30am Fri, 7.30pm-3am Sat, 7pm-1am Sun 🚉 🚌 ⛴ Circular Quay

Empire Hotel (2, B5) The Empire's well-managed 300-capacity bar gets down 'n' dirty with some of Sydney's best blues and roots. Local bands with loyal followings (Psycho Zydeco, Hippos, Satellite 5) play free gigs; listen out for international artists and regular rockabilly and country-and-western nights.
☎ 9557 1701 🖳 www.empirehotelsydney.com ✉ cnr Parramatta Rd & Johnston St, Annandale 💲 free-$10 🕑 10am-3pm Wed-Sat, to midnight Sun-Tue

🚉 Stanmore 🚌 413, 435-8, 440, 461 ♿ fair

Enmore Theatre (2, B5)
Originally a vaudeville playhouse, the charmingly faded Enmore now hosts acts like Lou Reed, PJ Harvey and Luka Bloom as well as theatre and comedy. The 1600-capacity theatre feels like an old-time movie hall, with café, wooden floors, lounge areas and balconies.
☎ 9550 3666 🖳 www.enmoretheatre.com.au ✉ 130 Enmore Rd, Newtown 💲 20-60 🕑 box office 9am-6pm Mon-Fri 🚉 Newtown 🚌 355, 370, 422-3, 426, 428 ♿ good 🚸 school holiday events

Hopetoun Hotel (6, A5)
Once the uncontested crucible for every new rock band, the diminutive 'Hoey' is still a launch pad for garage bands on the boil. Sunday afternoon it transforms into a chill-out space with DJs and all-night party crawlers knocking the froth off a few cold ones

before they hit the sack.
☎ 9361 5257; fax 9331
8145 ✉ 416 Bourke
St, Surry Hills 💲 5-15
🕑 noon-midnight
Mon-Sat, to 10pm Sun
🚊 🚉 Central

Metro (5, C8) The Metro
must be a frontrunner for
'Sydney's Rockingest Rock
Venue' trophy. Big-name
indie bands like the Dandy
Warhols, well-chosen local
acts like the Sleepy Jackson,
and international DJs
lend weight to the cause.
Theatre-style tiers, air con,
good sound and visibility
spell r-o-c-k ROCK!
☎ 9287 2000 🖥 www
.metrotheatre.com.au
✉ 624 George St 💲 25-
50 🕑 box office 10am-
7pm Mon-Fri, noon-7pm
Sat 🚉 Town Hall Ⓜ City
Centre 🚌 George St
buses ♿ fair

Side On Cafe (2, B5)
Slide on into the Side On, a
veritable jazz/arts hub and
restaurant regularly showcas-
ing Sydney's finest modern
jazz singers and players.
Bernie McGann, Mike Nock
and Sandy Evans regularly
keep the hep cats' fingers
a-snappin' while the cinema
upstairs screens quirky retro-
spectives and short films.
☎ 9516 3077 🖥 www
.side-on.com.au ✉ 83
Parramatta Rd, Annan-
dale 💲 15+ (varies)
🕑 7pm-midnight
🚉 Stanmore 🚌 413,
435-8, 440, 461

Soup Plus (5, C6) City
jazzniks cram into this
sweaty, low, basement
soup restaurant to dig

mostly mainstream jazz.
Monthly jam sessions
feature everything from
trad to bop, but most
nights it's raucous office
parties shaking the boss
off their backs to contemporary rhythms. Bookings
are advised; berets are
optional.
☎ 9299 7728 🖥 www
.soupplus.com.au ✉ 383
George St 💲 5-8 Mon-
Thu, dinner & show $28
Fri & Sat 🕑 noon-mid-
night Mon-Sat 🚉 Town
Hall Ⓜ City Centre
🚌 George St buses

**Sydney Entertainment
Centre (5, C8)** Sydney's

largest indoor stadium
venue holds over 12,000
howling rock fans, recent
acts including David Bowie,
Incubus, Radiohead and
James Brown. Its padded
purple seats also fill with
kids going nuts for the Wig-
gles and Bob the Builder,
and it's also the home court
of the Sydney Kings and
Flames basketball teams.
☎ 9320 4200 🖥 www
.sydentcent.com.au
✉ 35 Harbour St,
Haymarket 💲 varies
🕑 box office 9am-5pm
Mon-Fri 🚉 Central
Ⓜ Powerhouse Museum
🚉 Haymarket ♿ good
🧒 school holiday events

The Enmore Theatre – tasty entertainment

DANCE CLUBS

DCM (6, A3) Hard-core dance fans of all persuasions bust down DCM's doors on weekends. It's cookin' after 3am, with scantily clad clubbers posturing on podiums and reclining in multiple chill-out rooms. The cloakroom's cavernous – wear as much or as little as you like. ☎ 9267 7380 ✉ 335 Oxford St, Darlinghurst 💲 15-25 🕙 10pm-6am Fri, 10pm-10am Sat, to 8am Sun 🚇 Museum 🚌 378, 380, 382, L82

Gas (5, D9) Ground Zero for sexy young thangs shaking it up all weekend. The music crosses the canyons from hip-hop, R&B and soul (Thursday) to funkin' house (Friday) and trance and hard house (Saturday). Heart-start the night with a few shots at **Bohem**, the schmoove bar upstairs. ☎ 9211 3088 💻 www .gasnightclub.com .au ✉ 477 Pitt St, Haymarket 💲 15-30 🕙 10pm-6am Thu-Sat 🚉 🚉 Central 🚌 George St buses

Goodbar (6, B4) Looking for Mr Goodbar? If he's hiding in this tiny club, it won't take you long to flush him out. No luck? Console yourself with Thursday night's 'Step Forward' – funk, soul, reggae and hip-hop amongst the taut Paddo bods who make it past the face police on the door. ☎ 9360 6759 ✉ 11a Oxford St, Paddington

💲 5-10 🕙 9pm-3am Wed-Sat 🚌 378, 380, 382, L82

home (5, C6) Welcome to the pleasuredome: home's three-level, 2000-capacity timber and glass 'prow' is home to a huge dance floor, countless bars, outdoor balconies and sonics that make other clubs sound like transistor radios. Catch top-name UK and US DJs spinning a smorgasbord of deep house, breaks, techno, garage and funk. ☎ 9266 0600 💻 www .homesydney.com.au ✉ Cockle Bay Wharf, Darling Harbour 💲 25 🕙 11pm-6am Fri & Sat 🚇 Town Hall Ⓜ Darling Park 🚢 Darling Harbour ♿ fair

Slip Inn (5, C5) Slip in to this warren of moody rooms and bump hips with the cool kids. Resident and international selectors mix up old-school funk, latin grooves, breaks, tech and house. Refuel with pizza in the Sand Bar or Thai in the Garden Bar. All whims indulged. ☎ 8297 7000 💻 www .merivale.com ✉ 111 Sussex St 💲 free-15 🕙 5.30pm-2am Thu, 10pm-4am Fri, 8pm-4am Sat 🚇 Wynyard Ⓜ Darling Park 🚢 Darling Harbour

Tank (5, D4) They've got a VIP room – the question is, are you 'I' enough? Muster tank-loads of

Kylie cuts the rug

glamour and buckets of chutzpah and crash the private room (hey, aren't you Brad Pitt?). Otherwise, mingle with *waaay*-too-young stockbrokers and their waif girlfriends in this world-class, under-earth club. ☎ 9240 3007 💻 www .tankclub.com.au ✉ 3 Bridge La 💲 15/20 Fri/Sat 🕙 10.30pm-5am Fri & Sat 🚉 🚉 🚢 Circular Quay

Yu (6, C2) Debut the sassy new you at Yu. Sydney's best house DJs and vocal MCs (MC Fro) spin hip-hop, nu-skool, vocal and funky house in three rooms divided by sliding video screen doors. Sunday's 'After Hours' kicks till you jezz can't take no mo'. ☎ 9358 65117 💻 www .yu.com.au ✉ 171 Victoria St 💲 15/20/10 Fri/Sat/Sun 🕙 10pm-6am Fri-Sun 🚉 Kings Cross 🚌 330, 323-7, 365, 366, 389, L24

CINEMAS

Academy Twin Cinema (6, B4) Arthouse enthusiasts roll up for Academy's broad selection of independent Australian and international releases and the annual **Mardi Gras Film Festival** in March. Just down the street the **Verona Cinema** (6, B4; ☎ 9360 6099; 17 Oxford St) has similar fare, opening hours and prices. ☎ 9331 3457 🖳 www .palace.net.au ✉ 3a Oxford St, Paddington 💲 14.50/11 🕑 11am-9.30pm 🚌 378, 380, 382, L82

Dendy Opera Quays (5, F3) When the harbour glare and squawking of seagulls gets too much, duck into the dark folds of this plush cinema. One of several Dendys around Sydney screening first-run, independent world films, augmented by friendly attendants, a café and a bar. ☎ 9247 3800 🖳 www .dendy.com.au ✉ Shop 9, 2 Circular Quay East 💲 14/10.50 🕑 10.30am-9.45pm 🚉 🚌 🚢 Circular Quay 🚻 fair

Greater Union Hoyts Cinemas (5, C7) This movie behemoth combines three large cinema complexes in an orgy of popcorn-fuelled mainstream cinematography. They've got more screens than you can poke a stick at, plus special 'crybaby' sessions for the extra young (or just fractious). ☎ 9273 7373 🖳 www .hoyts.com.au ✉ 505-23 George St 💲 14.80/11.30 🕑 9.30am-midnight

🚉 Town Hall Ⓜ World Square 🚉 Capitol Square 🚌 George St buses 🚻 good

IMAX Cinema (5, B7) It's big bucks for a 45min movie, but everything about IMAX is big. The eight-storey screen shimmers with a selection of kid-friendly documentaries (nature, sports and adventure), many in 3-D, that reluctantly win over adults as well. Size matters. ☎ 9281 3300 🖳 www .imax.com.au ✉ Southern Promenade, Darling Harbour 💲 17/14 🕑 10am-10pm 🚉 Town Hall Ⓜ Darling Park 🚉 Convention 🚢 Darling Harbour 🚻 good

Moonlight Cinema (6, F6) A mellow way to enjoy a balmy summer evening: bring a rug, a picnic and a mate. The programme includes classics like *Breakfast at Tiffany's*, *Ferris Bueller's Day Off* and *A Clockwork Orange*. Bookings through Ticketek (☎ 9266 4800),

or buy tickets at the gate from 7pm. ☎ 1900 933 899 🖳 www.moonlight.com .au ✉ Centennial Park, Oxford St (Woollahra Gate) 💲 14.50/11.50 🕑 dusk, late Nov–early Mar 🚉 Bondi Junction 🚌 378, 380, 382, 389, L82 🚻 🚻 fair

Open Air Cinema (2, C4) Outdoor summer cinema done with aplomb: a three-storey screen, surround-sound and a 1700-seat grandstand distract the crowd from harbour sunsets. Nosh before you watch with swanky food and wine. Bookings essential. **Bondi Open Air Cinema** (3, B1; ☎ 9209 4614; www .bondiopenair.com.au; Bondi Pavilion) is similar but saltier. ☎ 1300 366 649 🖳 www .stgeorge.com.au/openair ✉ Mrs Macquaries Pt, Royal Botanic Gardens 💲 18/16.50 🕑 box office 6.30pm, screenings 8.30pm Jan-Feb 🚉 🚌 🚢 Circular Quay 🚻

THEATRE & COMEDY

Company B (2, C5) Artistic director Neil Armfield is the darling of the Sydney theatre world. Cinema stars like Geoffrey Rush clamour to perform his adventurous interpretations of modern masters like David Hare and Sam Shepard in two theatres: 80 seats downstairs, 320 up. Bookings advisable.

☎ 9667 3444 ⌨ www .belvoir.com.au ✉ Belvoir Street Theatre, 25 Belvoir St, Surry Hills $ 45/30 🕐 box office 9.30am-6pm Mon-Sat, to 7.30pm Wed-Sat, 2.30-7.30pm Sun 🚇 🚉 Central ♿ fair

Rhythmboat Comedy Cruise (5, B6) This four-hour harbour cruise combines stand-up comedy and magic with a three-course meal and a live Caribbean band. Suffocating fits of belly laughter aren't guaranteed, but the Harbour Bridge views will bring a tear to your eye. Good for groups.

☎ 9879 3942 ⌨ www .rhythmboat.com.au ✉ Pyrmont Bay Wharf $ 65 ($55 groups of

Is she really going out with him? Find out at the State Theatre (p89)

12+) 🕐 7.15-11.30pm Sat Ⓜ Harbourside 🚉 Pyrmont Bay 🚢 Pyrmont Bay

Stables Theatre (6, C3) In the 19th century this place was knee-high in horse dung; now it's home to the critically acclaimed Griffin Theatre Co, dedicated to nurturing new writers and performing experimental works by contemporary Australian playwrights. Book at the Opera House or at the theatre one hour before shows.

☎ 9250 7799 ⌨ www .griffintheatre.com.au ✉ 10 Nimrod St, Darlinghurst $ 18-35 🕐 Opera

House box office 9am-8.30pm Mon-Fri 🚉 Kings Cross 🚌 323-7, 324-5, 333, 389

Sydney Comedy Store (2, D5) This purpose-built comedy hall lures big-time Australian and overseas stand-ups and nurtures new talent with open mic and 'New Comics' nights. Irish acts and Edinburgh Festival performers have 'em rolling in the aisles on a regular basis. Bookings advisable.

☎ 9357 1419 ⌨ www .comedystore.com.au ✉ Fox Studios, Driver Ave, Moore Park $ 15 Tue-Thu, $27.50 Fri & Sat 🕐 box office 10am-6pm

Star City Casino

Decorated in a 'Disney Goes Outback' theme, Star City Casino (5, A6; ☎ 9777 9000; www.starcity.com.au; 80 Pyrmont , Pyrmont; free; 🕐 24hr; Ⓜ Harbourside; 🚢 Pyrmont Bay) is a sprawling maze of less, air-conditioned money. There's a ing rooms with more than 200 bet-rants, shops, bars and the large, tre.

Mon, 10am-midnight
Tue-Sat 🚌 371-4, 376-7
♿ fair

Sydney Theatre (5, C3)
Opening in January 2004
with a name it seems odd
no-one's thought of before,
the resplendent Sydney
Theatre puts 850 bums on
seats for specialist drama
and dance. The Monday-to-
Thursday evening 'Student
Rush' offers $17 tickets
(first come/first served).
Have dinner at **Hickson
Rd Bistro** before the
curtain rises.
☎ 9250 1999 🖳 www
.sydneytheatre.org.au
✉ 22 Hickson Rd, Walsh
Bay 💲 63/51/17 🕙 box
office 9am-8.30pm
🚆 🚢 Circular Quay
🚌 430-4 ♿ good, call
for info

Exit, Stage L...
Major theatres host...
sicals, opera and conc...
Capitol Theatre (5, D...
itoltheatre.com.au; 13 C...
State Theatre (5, D6; ☎ ... ...www.state
theatre.com.au; 4 Market St)
Theatre Royal (5, D6; ☎ 9266 4800; www.mlc
centre.com.au/public/index.htm; MLC Centre, 108
King St)
Check media for current shows.

Sydney Theatre Company
(5, C2) Working in tandem
with the larger Sydney Theatre across the road, the STC
is Sydney's premier theatre
company. Major Australian
actors (Barry Otto, Deborah
Mailman) perform works by
Alan Bennet, David Wil-
liamson and Shakespeare.
Smaller, more experimental
works play the Wharf, bigger
shows play the Sydney
Theatre and Opera House.
☎ 9250 1777 🖳 www
.sydneytheatre.com.au
✉ Pier 4, 5 Hickson Rd,
Walsh Bay 💲 63/51/17
🕙 box office 9am-8.30pm
🚆 🚢 Circular Quay
🚌 430-4 ♿ good, call
for info 🚹 some events

INDIGENOUS PERFORMANCE

Dance and song are an important part of Australia's Aboriginal and
Torres Strait Islander cultures, the stories they express informed by spiritual ancestors and links with the land (see **Aboriginal Art** p31).

Bangarra Dance Company
(5, C2) Bangarra is hailed
as Australia's finest Aboriginal dance company. Artistic
director Stephen Page
conjures a fusion of the
contemporary and the indigenous, blending traditional
Torres Strait Islander dance
with Western technique.
Bookings essential.
☎ 9251 5333 🖳 www
.bangarra.com.au ✉ Pier
4, 5 Hickson Rd, Walsh
Bay; performances at
**Theatre Royal and Opera
House** 💲 20-50 🕙 call
for performance details
♿ call for info 🚹

NAISDA (5, D3) Driven by a
philosophy of preservation,
constructive education and
celebration of indigenous
dance culture, the National
Aboriginal & Islander Skills
Development Association
performing arts college
presents biannual performances incorporating dance,
song and spoken word. Call
for details and to book.
☎ 9252 0199 🖳 www
.naisda.com.au ✉ 3
Cumberland St, The
Rocks 💲 15-20 🕙 call
for performance details
🚆 🚌 🚢 Circular Quay
🚹

Yiribana Gallery (5, D3)
Surrounded by the Yiribana
Gallery's stunning collection
of Aboriginal art (don't
miss *Tingari Story* by Willy
Tjungurrayi and *Hunting
Grounds* by Pantjiti Mary
McLean), see indigenous
performers dance, sing and
tell stories at these free,
40min shows.
☎ 9225 1744 🖳 www
.artgallery.nsw.gov
.au ✉ Art Gallery of
NSW, Art Gallery Rd,
The Domain 💲 free
🕙 noon Tue-Sat
🚆 St James 🚌 200
♿ good 🚹

...ty Recital Hall (5, D5) Based on the classical configuration of the 19th-century European concert hall, this custom-built 1200-seat venue boasts near-perfect acoustics. Catch top-flight companies like Musica Viva, the Australian Brandenburg and Chamber Orchestras, the Sydney Symphony and touring international ensembles, soloists and opera singers. ☎ 8256 2222 ▢ www .cityrecitalhall.com ✉ 2-12 Angel Pl, Sydney $ free-60 ☉ box office 9am-5pm Mon-Fri ▣ Martin Place, Wynyard Ⓜ City Centre ♿ good

Conservatorium of Music (5, E4) 'The Con' has a history of bulbous building costs. The $145 million spent recently refurbished its five live venues. The annual student/teacher performance programme includes choral, jazz, operatic and chamber recitals, free lunchtime concerts and lectures. ☎ 9351 1342 ▢ www .usyd.edu.au/su/conmusic ✉ cnr Macquarie & Bridge Sts $ free-25 ☉ box office 9am-5pm Mon-Fri ▣ Circular Quay, Martin Place ▣ ▣ Circular Quay ♿ good

The Domain (5, E6) Each summer, thousands stuff a picnic hamper and truck over to The Domain for free twilight concerts. The three most popular happen in January: Opera Australia's **Opera in the Park** (☎ 9319 1088), Sydney Symphony's **Symphony in the Domain** (☎ 9334 4644) and the Sydney Festival's **Jazz in the Domain** (☎ 8248 6500). **Carols by Candlelight** twinkles here every Christmas Eve. ✉ The Domain, Sydney ▣ Martin Place, St James ▣ 411, 200 ♿ good ♿

Sydney Dance Company (5, C2) Under the direction of its inexhaustible choreographer Graeme Murphy, the SDC is Australia's No 1 contemporary dance company. For over 25 years Murphy has boogied-up the nation's cultural psyche with his wildly modern, sexy, sometimes shocking works. Cut the rug with a SDC dance lesson for $16! ☎ 9221 4811 ▢ www .sydneydance.com.au ✉ Pier 4, 5 Hickson Rd, Walsh Bay; performances at Capitol Theatre and Opera House $ 29-75 ☉ varies ▣ ▣ Circular Quay ▣ 430-4 ♿ good ♿

Sydney Opera House (5, E2) The Concert Hall and Opera Theatre host the **Australian Ballet** (☎ 9252 5500), **Australian Chamber Orchestra** (☎ 8274 3800), **Opera Australia** (☎ 9319 1088), **Musica Viva** (☎ 8694 6666), **Sydney Dance Company** (left), **Sydney Philharmonic Choirs** (☎ 9251 2024) and **Sydney Symphony** (☎ 9334 4644). The **Sydney Theatre Company** (p89) plays the Drama Theatre; **Bell Shakespeare** (☎ 9241 2722) shakes the Playhouse. ☎ 9250 7777 ▢ www .sydneyoperahouse .com.au ✉ Bennelong Pt, Circular Quay East $ varies ☉ box office 9am-8.30pm Mon-Sat, 2½ hr pre-show Sun ▣ ▣ ▣ Circular Quay ♿ good ♿ Kids at the House programme

Roll Over Beethoven

Universities hold regular classical recitals. The **Great Hall** (2, B5; ☎ 9351 2949; Sydney University) hosts the esteemed Chamber Choir, University Musical Society and Graduate Choir. The Australia Ensemble and Collegium Musicum choir and orchestra cut loose at **John Clancy Auditorium** (2, D6; ☎ 9385 4874; University of NSW).

Several of Sydney's churches present classical concerts and recitals, including **St Andrew's Cathedral** (5, C7; ☎ 9265 1661; cnr George & Bathurst Sts); **St James Church** (5, E6; ☎ 9232 3022; Queens Sq), **St Philip's Church** (5, C4; ☎ 9247 1071; 3 York St) and **St Stephen's Church** (5, E5; ☎ 9221 1688; 197 Macquarie St). Call for details.

GAY & LESBIAN SYDNEY

Sydney's reputation as a gay cultural hot pot has long been established, thanks to events like Mardi Gras and films like *Priscilla, Queen of the Desert*. Newtown and Taylor Sq in Darlinghurst are the main gay drags with bars, clubs and restaurants for all facets of gay culture.

Arq (6, B4) If Noah had to fill his bilge with groovy, gay clubbers, he'd head here with a big net and some tranquillisers. This flash megaclub has a cocktail bar, recovery room and two dance floors with hi-energy house, drag shows and a hyperactive smoke machine. ☎ 9380 8700 ▯ www .arqsydney.com.au ✉ 16 Flinders St, Darlinghurst 💲 Thu/Fri/Sat/Sun free/10/20/5 🕑 9pm-6am Thu & Fri, 10pm-9am Sat, 9pm 9am Sun 🚌 3/8, 380, 382, 182 ♿ fair

Californian (6, B4) It's a hazy 5am. You need a beer, a chicken burger and a flirty smile from a hunky waiter. Forget the YMCA young man, head to the Californian. Slide into a red booth or a footpath table and soak up Oxford Street's late-night leftovers. ☎ 9331 5587 ✉ 177 Oxford St, Darlinghurst 💲 free 🕑 24hr Wed-Sun, 8am-2am Mon-Tue 🚌 378, 380, 382, L82 ♿ footpath only

Imperial Hotel (2, B5) The Art Deco Imperial's drag shows inspired *Priscilla, Queen of the Desert* (the opening scene was filmed here). Any drag queen worth her sheen has played the Cabaret Room. The Cellar Bar, Public Bar and Priscilla Lounge heave with chesty pool boys and raging house.

☎ 9519 9899 ▯ www .theimperial.com.au ✉ 35 Erskineville Rd, Erskineville 💲 free 🕑 3pm-midnight, to 2.30am Thu, to 6am Fri & Sat 🚊 Newtown 🚌 355, 370, 422-3, 426, 428

Lord Roberts Hotel (6, A3) The Lord Roberts is all things to all people: pub, cocktail bar, restaurant, bottle shop, pool hall and function room with DJs from Thursday to Sunday. Sunday afternoons' lesbian crush elbows around the pool tables. ☎ 9360 9555 ▯ www .lordrobertshotel.com.au ✉ 64 Stanley St, East

Sydney 💲 free 🕑 10am-midnight 🚊 Museum

Midnight Shift (6, A3) Sydney's perennial good-time boy palace (a.k.a. the Midnight Shirtlift) packs in everyone from beefcakes to drags. The grog is cheap, the patrons messy, Kylie rules and mankind chalks its collective cue by the pool tables. ☎ 9360 4319 ▯ www .themidnightshift.com ✉ 85 Oxford St, Darlinghurst 💲 free 🕑 video bar noon-late Mon-Fri, 2pm-late Sat & Sun; nightclub 11pm-late Fri & Sat 🚌 378, 380, 382, L82

Stonewall Hotel: lady, erm, man in red

Newtown Hotel (2, B5)
The Newtown does a heady gay trade with folks who just want to go to the local boozer and have a few laughs. Musical stimulation is provided by the sensational sequined drag acts like Portia Turbo and Pru Crimson.
☎ 9557 1329 🖳 www .newtownhotel.com
✉ 174 King St, Newtown ⑤ free 🕑 11am-midnight Mon-Fri, 10am-midnight Sat, to 10pm Sun
🚃 Newtown 🚌 355, 370, 422-3, 426, 428
♿ fair

Odyssey (6, B4) When you drag your bones out of bed at whatever pm, boot it down to Odyssey for a beer, some tapas and a perv over Taylor Sq. The cocktail bar fires up later on with barmen and national-standard DJs like Kate Monroe.
☎ 9360 3388
🖳 accounts@odyssey -lounge.com ✉ 191 Oxford St, Taylor Sq, Darlinghurst ⑤ free 🕑 restaurant 10.30am-11pm,

bar 6pm-late 🚌 378, 380, 382, L82 ♿ excellent

Oxford Hotel (6, B4) Big, swollen and crimson, the ever-lovin' Oxford is a Taylor Sq beacon. The ground floor is beer-swilling and mannish. First-floor Gilligan's serves luxe cocktails and top-floor Ginger's has indulgent lounge service. After-dance party crowds heave and sway.
☎ 9331 3467 ✉ 134 Oxford St, Taylor Sq, Darlinghurst ⑤ free 🕑 24hr downstairs, Gilligans 5pm-late, Ginger's 6pm-late Thu-Sat 🚌 378, 380, 382, L82

Phoenix Bar (6, A3)
Affiliated with **Q Bar** (☎ 9360 1375) upstairs, Phoenix is the sticky, sexy, claustrophobic home to an alternative gay crowd sweating in the darkness to hard house. Grungy to the hilt and packed solid on weekends.
☎ 9331 1936 🖳 www .qbar.com.au ✉ Basement, 34 Oxford St, Darlinghurst ⑤ Thu/Fri/

Sat free/5/10 🕑 10pm-6am Thu-Sat 🚌 378, 380, 382, L82

Stonewall Hotel (6, B4)
Nicknamed 'Stonehenge' by those who think it's archaic (gay druids?), the Stonewall has three levels of bars and dance floors. Cabaret and games nights spice things up – Wednesday's 'Malebox' is a sure-fire way to bag yourself a boy.
☎ 9360 1963 🖳 www .stonewallhotel.com
✉ 175 Oxford St, Darlinghurst ⑤ free 🕑 11am-6am 🚌 378, 380, 382, L82

Tool Shed (6, A3) Need a cock ring, some handcuffs or a ticket to a mega-dance party (or maybe all three)? Get your butt over to the Tool Shed, a sex shop and ticketing agent. Also at Taylor Sq and 196 King St, Newtown.
☎ 9332 2792 🖳 www .toolshed.com.au ✉ 81 Oxford St, Darlinghurst 🕑 10am-1am, to 3am Fri & Sat 🚌 378, 380, 382, L82

Mardi Gras

Started in 1978 as a political march to commemorate New York's Stonewall riots, Mardi Gras has evolved into a month-long arts festival culminating in a flesh-coloured street parade and party on the last Saturday in February. The gyms empty out, the solariums cool down, 'back, sack and crack' wax emporiums tally their profits and you can't hire a costume for quids.

The parade – a rampant procession of up to 200 floats – begins on the corner of Elizabeth and Liverpool Sts around 7.30pm, and prances the length of Oxford St before trundling down Flinders St, Moore Park Rd and Driver Ave to the old Sydney Showgrounds. If you want to be among the 700,000 or so watching the parade, find some friends with a balcony view of Oxford St or cordon off a patch of pavement several hours before it starts. Bring a milk crate to stand on (oh-so-suddenly scarce) and take some water with you.

Call the festival hotline ☎ 9568 8600 or check out www.mardigras.org.au for the lowdown.

SPORTS

You'll find vociferous crowds and world-class athletes in action on every weekend of the year in Sydney.

Basketball

Australia's basketball league has all the razzmatazz of US pro basketball (and quite a few US players) and is massively popular with kids and teenagers. The basketball season runs from April to November, games played on weekends at the **Sydney Entertainment Centre** (5, C8). The Sydney teams are the **Flames** (women, NWBL) and the **Kings** (men, NBL). Contact the **NSW Basketball Association** (☎ 9746 2969; www .nbl.com.au, www.nwbl.com.au) for details.

Cricket

The **Sydney Cricket Ground** is home to sparsely attended Pura Cup matches (interstate), well-attended Test matches (international) and sell-out World Series Cup matches (one-day international). Australia dominates both international forms of the game. Local district games are also played here, the cricket season running from October to March. Check www.baggygreen.com.au for information.

Aussie, Aussie, Aussie... Oi, Oi, Oi!

Football

Australian Rules Football is a unique, skilful and awe-inspiring sport – only Gaelic football comes close to it. The **Sydney Swans** are NSW's only contribution to the **Australian Football League** (AFL; www.afl.com.au; tickets $20-40). See the big men fly at the 40,000-seat Sydney Cricket Ground and Telstra Stadium. The AFL season runs from March to September.

Soccer is gaining popularity, thanks in part to the success of the national team, the **Socceroos**, and to the crop of high-profile Australian stars playing overseas. The National Soccer League (NSL) is semi-professional, games attracting small but enthusiastic crowds. Contact **Soccer Australia** (☎ 9739 5555; www.australiansoccer.com.au) for information.

Rugby

Sydney is one of the world capitals of **rugby league**. The main competition (including interstate sides) is the Telstra Premiership, run by the **National Rugby League** (NRL; www.nrl.com.au). Games are played at various grounds, but the sell-out finals happen in August/September (Aussie Stadium & Telstra Stadium; $15-25). The other big Rugby League series is the parochial passion inducing **State of Origin**, played annually between NSW and Queensland.

Rugby union (www.rugbyunion.com.au) has a less fanatical following but is gaining converts. Australia hosted the 2003 World Cup, the Australian team (2003 runners-up) the **Wallabies** featuring some high-profile defectors from rugby league. See them in action against international teams in Sydney periodically.

Surf Lifesaving

The volunteer surf lifesaver is one of Australia's cultural icons, but despite macho imagery, many surf lifesavers these days are female. You can see lifesavers in action each summer at surf carnivals held all along the coast. Check at local surf lifesaving clubs for dates or contact **Surf Life Saving NSW** (☎ 9130 7370; www.slsa.asn.au).

Tennis

The **Adidas International** tennis tournament is held in the second week of January as a prelude to the Australian Open in Melbourne. It's on at the Sydney International Tennis Centre. Book through Ticketek (☎ 9266 4800; www.ticketek.com). Call **Tennis NSW** (☎ 9763 7644) for local tournament information.

Yachting

On weekends, hundreds of yachts tack and bob around the ferries and ships on Sydney Harbour. The speedy 18ft skiff racing season runs from mid-September to late March, race winners cashing in on healthy

> ### Major Sports Venues
> **Aussie Stadium** (6, C6; ☎ 9360 6601; Driver Ave, Moore Park)
>
> **Sydney Cricket Ground** (6, C6; ☎ 9360 6601; Driver Ave, Moore Park)
>
> **Sydney International Tennis Centre** (1, D2; ☎ 8746 0777; Homebush Bay Dr, Homebush Bay)
>
> **Telstra Stadium** (1, D2; ☎ 8765 2000; Olympic Blvd, Homebush Bay)

Telstra Stadium – Olympic proportions

prize money. The oldest and largest 18-footer club is the **Sydney Flying Squadron** (2, C3; ☎ 9955 8350; www.sydneyflyingsquadron.com.au; 76 McDougall St, Milsons Point; $15/5.50; ☼ 2-4.30pm; ☂). Catch a ferry from here to see Saturday skiff racing between September and April. Sydney Harbour's greatest yachting event is the Boxing Day (26 December) start of the harrowing **Sydney to Hobart Yacht Race**. The harbour jams up with competitors, media boats and a huge spectator armada. Special ferries are scheduled by Sydney Ferries to follow the yachts; call ☎ 13 15 00 in November for ticket information.

30ft or 8ft, there's no place like Sydney Harbour for messing about in boats

Sleeping

You'll have no problem finding a place to lay your head in Sydney, with solid options in every price range. During the busy summer months, most hotels and hostels increases room rates and cancel any prior promotional deals. Conversely, when tumbleweeds blow through lobbies in the slower winter months, you can often strike a bargain. Booking through an accommodation agency like **Tourism NSW** (☎ 13 20 77; www.tourism .nsw.gov.au) can sometimes land you a discount.

Mid-range to deluxe hotels publish 'rack' rates (standard rates) but it's worth ringing ahead to see if there are any current specials. Many hotels cater primarily to business people, so their rates may be lower on weekends. Breakfast and on-site parking is sometimes included in the room price. Predictably, a view can play a big part in determining the price of a Sydney room.

If you're bunking down in budget lodgings, Sydney has plenty of hostels, pubs and guesthouses. Facilities range from basic dorms to well-kept rooms with en suite, TV and shared kitchens.

Serviced apartments, which offer hotel-style convenience plus self-catering cooking facilities can be good value, especially for families. They vary in size from hotel rooms with a bar fridge and microwave to full-blown three-bedroom apartments.

Between November and February, prices at beachside resorts can be as much as 40% higher. Inner-city hotels, serviced apartments and Bed & Breakfasts (B&Bs) have a 10% goods and services tax (GST) included in the price.

Room Rates

The price ranges in this chapter indicate the cost per night of a standard double room:

Deluxe	over $350
Top End	$250-350
Mid-Range	$125-249
Budget	under $125

W Hotel Sydney: Woolloomooloo never looked so swish

DELUXE

Establishment (5, D4) So hip it hurts, Establishment is the secret hideaway for superstars and squillionaires (not so secret now, eh?) with the coolest interior design in town – exquisite furnishings, indulgent bathrooms and high-tech services proliferate. **Tank** nightclub (p86), **Est.** restaurant (p68) and **Tank Stream**, **Establishment** and **Hemmesphere** bars (p82 and p83) are on site.
☎ 9240 3100 🖳 www
.establishmenthotel
.com ✉ 5 Bridge La
🚇 🚌 🚢 Circular
Quay ♿ fair ✖ bars,
restaurant

Four Points Sheraton (5, C6) A curvilinear white façade and stylish rooms make this the most aesthetically competent of the Darling Harbour hotel monoliths. Conventioneers and business bods appreciate the limo service, airport shuttle, fitness and function centres.
☎ 9290 4000 🖳 www
.fourpoints.com ✉ 161

Sussex St 🚇 Wynyard, Town Hall 🚊 Darling Park 🚢 Darling Harbour 🅿 ♿ fair ✖ bars, restaurants 🚼

Four Seasons (5, D4) The Four Seasons oozes class – extraordinarily professional staff, knockout views (city, Opera House or harbour – take your pick), Sydney's largest rooftop pool and ballroom, 24-hour gym, day spa, live music, attentive concierge and little extras like daily shoe shine. Go on, you know you deserve it…
☎ 9238 0000 🖳 www
.fourseasons.com/sydney/
✉ 199 George St, The
Rocks 🚇 🚌 🚢 Circular
Quay 🅿 ♿ good
✖ restaurants, bars 🚼

Observatory Hotel (5, C3) Marble bathrooms, monogrammed robes, feather quilts, 24-hour room service – the Observatory is opulent to the soul. After your complimentary (for overseas travellers) float-tank session at the

day spa, sip a G&T or three in the Globe Bar. Lined with leather-bound books, the vibe is 'country aristocrats' den'.
☎ 9256 2222 🖳 www
.observatoryhotel.com
.au ✉ 89-113 Kent St,
Milsons Point 🚇 Circular
Quay, Wynyard 🚌 339,
430-4 🚢 Circular Quay
🅿 ♿ good ✖ bar,
restaurants

Park Hyatt (5, D2) Facing off with the Opera House and within spitting distance of the Harbour Bridge, the curvaceous Park Hyatt is super-luxurious and super-located. Rooms boast Internet TV access and marble baths, there's a rooftop pool with Jacuzzi and – if your socks need darning at 4am – a 24-hour butler service.
☎ 9241 1234 🖳 www
.sydney.hyatt.com ✉ 7
Hickson Rd, The Rocks
🚇 🚌 🚢 Circular Quay
♿ good ✖ bar, restaurants

Sheraton on the Park (5, D6) The Sheraton recently tired of its interiors and had a design crew sweep the broom through every room. The results are difficult to fault, and with gym, indoor pool, Hyde Park views and wireless Internet in every room, it's quite possible this place *is* faultless.
☎ 9286 6000 🖳 www
.sheraton.com.au ✉ 161
Elizabeth St 🚇 St James,
Town Hall 🚊 City Centre
🅿 ♿ good
✖ restaurants, bar 🚼

The Four Points Sheraton points to the sky (that's it on the left!)

TOP END

Hotel InterContinental
(5, E4) Emerging like a phoenix from the noble sandstone buildings once housing the Treasury, the InterContinental has got what it takes. All 70 immaculate rooms have spa and balcony, while the rooftop Club Lounge has an outdoor garden terrace, grand piano, wireless Internet work areas, plasma TV and smokin' harbour views.
☎ 9253 9000 ▢ www
.sydney.intercontinental
.com ✉ 117 Macquarie
St 🚆 🚌 🚢 Circular
Quay 🅿 ♿ good
✖ restaurants, bar 🈯

Manly Pacific (4, B2)
Right on Manly's ocean beach, this dapper mid-rise hotel is 15 minutes by JetCat from Circular Quay and a million miles from the city's withering hustle. Check the surf from oceanfront balconies, or there's a rooftop pool if you don't want to get sand in your lap top.
☎ 9977 7666 ▢ www
.novotel.com.au ✉ 55
North Steyne, Manly
🚌 151, 169, E69
🚢 Manly 🅿 ♿ good
✖ restaurants, bar 🈯

Shangri-La Hotel (5, C4)
Try to contain your glee as you waltz into the Shangri-La, floating high above James Hilton's *Lost Horizon* on a silver-lined cloud. The salubrious lobby drips steadily with mesmeric waterfalls, scarlet-clad bellhops hop to it and the walls ooze cheesy, marbled, Las

Nice place for a glass of water: the Water Bar at the W Hotel

Vegas schmaltz. Shangri-La it just may be…
☎ 9250 6000 ▢ www
.shangri-la.com ✉ 176
Cumberland St, The Rocks
🚆 🚌 🚢 Circular Quay
🅿 ♿ good ✖ restaurants, bars

Sir Stamford at Circular Quay (5, E4)
Arise Sir Stamford, knight of the Circular Table. From this day forth, your antique furnishings, original artworks and chandeliers shall meld seamlessly with all mod-cons. Poised opposite the Royal Botanic Gardens, Sir would scream elegance, if screaming weren't so inelegant.
☎ 8274 5450 ▢ www
.stamford.com.au
✉ 93 Macquarie St
🚆 🚌 🚢 Circular Quay
🅿 ♿ fair ✖ restaurant, bar 🈯

W Hotel Sydney (6, B1)
The hotel rooms in Woolloomooloo's redeveloped wharf may be a bit poky but boutique sensibilities and gadgetry are redemptive. Hobnob with bigwigs and biz-kids at **Water Bar** (p83), relax at the day spa, cruise the wharf **restaurants** (p73) or sneak a peek at Russell Crowe's pad on the end of the pier.
☎ 9331 9000 ▢ www
.whotels.com ✉ 6
Cowper Wharf Rd,
Woolloomooloo
🚌 311 🅿 ♿ fair
✖ restaurants, bar

Westin (5, D5)
This gargantuan hotel (with executive services and fitness centre) is the corporate traveller's best mate. Book a 'heritage' room: the calm colour scheme, 4m-high ceiling and lavish bathroom with TV and deep-soaker tub will draw a hedonistic close to your business day. Very kid-friendly too.
☎ 8223 1111 ▢ www
.westin.com.au ✉ 1
Martin Pl 🚆 Martin
Place, Wynyard Ⓜ City
Centre 🅿 ♿ good
✖ cafés, restaurants,
bars 🈯

MID-RANGE

Blacket (5, C6) Beyond the chubby Buddha by the door, Blacket blends 'escape' with lashings of contemporary cool for just a dash of cash. Loft suites – all white, caramel and grey – sleep four and have spa, separate lounge, kitchenette and loads of whiz-bang doodahs (cable TV, CD players and data ports).
☎ 9279 3030 🖳 www .blackethotel.com.au ✉ 70 King St 🚇 Wyn-yard Ⓜ City Centre Ⓟ ♿ fair 🍽 café, bar, restaurant

Kirketon (6, B3) The Kir-keton's designer rooms are as impeccably turned out as the clientele. Stylishly sparse suites are jazzed up with ritzy toiletries, Lindt chocolates, mohair throw-rugs and plush bathrobes. **Salt** restaurant (p70) and **Fix** bar (p82) are world class.
☎ 9332 2011 🖳 www .kirketon.com.au ✉ 229 Darlinghurst Rd, Darling-hurst 🚇 Kings Cross

🚌 330, 323-7, 365, 366, 389, L24 🍽 restaurant, bar

Medusa (6, B3) Irresist-ible to designer darlings, Medusa's shocking-pink exterior merely hints at the witty, luscious décor inside. Small colour-saturated rooms boast enormous beds, mod-con bathrooms and regal furnishings. Ground-floor suites open onto a tranquil courtyard and reflection pool: meditation will minimise the chances of your hair turning into snakes. If it does, Medusa is very pet-friendly.
☎ 9331 1000 🖳 www .medusa.com.au ✉ 267 Darlinghurst Rd, Darlin-ghurst 🚇 Kings Cross 🚌 330, 323-7, 365, 366, 389, L24

Ravesi's (3, B2) Recently refurbished, Ravesi's fits into the Bondi scene like a briefcase on a beach, but the shaggy, salty surf-set might learn a thing or two from the suits drinking with

Russell on The Rocks

the supermodels at the bar. Upstairs, Ravesi's rooms are sophisticated, many with ocean views.
☎ 9365 4422 🖳 www .ravesis.com.au ✉ 118 Campbell Pde, Bondi Beach 🚌 380-2, L82 ♿ fair 🍽 bar, restaurant 🛇

Regent's Court (6, C2) This boutique Art Deco hotel in the leafy backblocks is big on personal service and mid-century furnish-ings. Handsome en-suite rooms come with impec-

Medusa the seducer

cably stocked kitchenettes, and the roof terrace with its Potts Point pot plants is an ace place for a barbeque. ☎ 9358 1533 ☐ www.regentscourt.com.au ✉ 18 Springfield Ave, Potts Point 🚇 Kings Cross 🚌 330, 323-7, 365, 366, 389, L24 Ⓟ 👤

Russell Hotel (5, D3) Traditionally decorated rooms (Laura Ashley, you have a lot to answer for), lounge areas with fireplaces, library and rooftop garden minutes from Circular Quay make this a top choice. Rooms have fresh flowers, and families can do what families do in the four-bed studio apartment. Continental breakfast included. ☎ 9241 3543 ☐ www.therussell.com.au ✉ 143a George St, The Rocks 🚇 🚌 🚢 Circular Quay ✘ restaurant 👤

Simpsons of Potts Point (6, C1) This 1892 politician's home has been faithfully rejuvenated and converted into a quiet, refined B&B. The

---

Hotels vs. Pubs

First-time visitors to Australia might be confused by the distinction between hotels and… well, hotels. There are three kinds.

Until relatively recently, any establishment serving alcohol was called a hotel and was legally required to provide accommodation (usually spartan and noisy). These hotels are also called **pubs** (public houses). **Private hotels** are boarding house–type places, similar to pubs but without a bar. They usually have the word 'private' in their names to distinguish them from the **hotels** you'll most probably be staying in – accommodation with extra facilities (room service, pool etc) usually rated at three stars or higher.

Got it? Now go to sleep.

---

14 rooms are spacious, with en suites (the Cloud Suite has a spa), fireplaces, balconies and antique prints. There's a large lounge with a piano if you want to mingle or tinkle. ☎ 9356 2199 ☐ www.simpsonshotel.com ✉ 8 Challis Ave, Potts Point 🚇 Kings Cross 🚌 330, 323-7, 365, 366, 389, L24 Ⓟ

Tricketts Bed & Breakfast (2, B4) Inside this preciously restored 1880s merchant's

mansion, seven large en-suite guest rooms are decked out with antiques and Persian rugs. The garden is a romantically verdant wonderland, there's a kitchen, ballroom, billiard table, porch and barbeque deck, continental breakfast is included and the atmosphere is decidedly non-Victorian. ☎ 9552 1141 ☐ www.tricketts.com.au ✉ 270 Glebe Point Rd, Glebe 🚌 431-4 🚇 Jubilee Park Ⓟ ✘ breakfast only

BUDGET

Bondi Beachouse YHA (3, B2) A short walk from the beach, Bondi Beachouse has clued-up staff, pool table, TV rooms, barbeque, free play stuff (surfboards, snorkels, etc) and rooftop views over Tamarama Beach from the spa. It's a friendly, clean, sunny-side-up kinda joint. En-suite doubles and family rooms available. ☎ 9365 2088 ☐ www.bondibeachouse.com.au

✉ 63 Fletcher St, Bondi Beach 🚌 380-2, L82 👤

Grand Hotel (5, D5) One of Sydney's oldest hotels, the Grand's first few floors jump with pokies, pool tables and beery hordes. Keep going up and you'll find neat rooms with TVs and fridges. Shared bathrooms can be a drag, but in this location for this price, you won't hear anyone

complaining. ☎ 9232 3755 ☐ grandhotel@merivale.com ✉ 30 Hunter St 🚇 Wynyard, Martin Place Ⓜ City Centre ✘ bistro

Hotel Altamont (6, B3) Altamont flagged the end of '60s peace and love, but here in Darlinghurst the good times continue unabated. Spiffy-looking doubles with bathrooms feel like they should cost more than they do, communal areas are welcoming (especially the terrace) and it's tantalisingly close to the Cross.

☎ 9360 6000 🖥 www .altamont.com.au ✉ 207 Darlinghurst Rd, Darlinghurst 🚇 Kings Cross 🚌 330, 323-7, 365, 366, 389, L24 🍴 bar 🚭

Palisade Hotel (5, B3) Improbably Gothic in its verticality and isolation, this old-time dock workers' pub has managed to dodge kitsch Rocks-style makeovers and remains a great place for a beer, a meal or a cheap night's sleep. Basic, clean upstairs rooms have shared bathrooms but munificent harbour views.

Hyde Park is a stone's throw from Y on the Park

☎ 9247 2272 🖥 www .palisadehotel.com ✉ 35 Bettington St, Millers Point 🚇 Wynyard, Circular Quay 🚌 431-4 ⛴ Circular Quay 🍴 bar, restaurant

Y on the Park (5, E8) The standards here are high – simple, spotless rooms with TV, phone, fridge and air con plus an adjoining café downstairs. The city centre is just beyond Hyde Park across the road and Oxford St is a wiggle away. Gets as busy as a woodpecker during Mardi Gras.

☎ 9264 2451 🖥 www .ywca-sydney.com.au ✉ 5-11 Wentworth Ave 🚇 Museum 🅿 ♿ good 🍴 café 🚭

SERVICED APARTMENTS

Manly Paradise (4, B1) Feel the salt on your skin at these comfortable apartments, sleeping five with balconies overlooking Manly ocean beach. There's a heated rooftop pool, spa, sauna, half-court tennis and cable TV. Cheaper motel-style rooms are available if you're feeling more 'road'.

☎ 9977 5799 🖥 www .manlyparadise.com .au ✉ 54 North Steyne 🚌 151, 169, E69 ⛴ Manly 🚭

Quay West (5, C4) Rumbling with the heavyweight hotels in this neck of the woods, these fine-looking serviced apartments (sorry, executive penthouses) have

views, kitchen, laundry and 24-hour room service. There's also a Romanesque swimming pool, spa, gym and sauna – sweat it out and pump it up.

☎ 9240 6000 🖥 www .mirvachotels.com.au ✉ 98 Gloucester St, The Rocks 🚇 🚌 ⛴ Circular Quay 🅿 ♿ fair 🍴 restaurant 🚭

Saville 2 Bond St (5, D5) If you're taking care of business, Saville will take care of you. Your room functions as an office with modem connection, CD player, safe, fax machine, cable news and financial channels and two phones for those number-crunching all-nighters. Free pool, gym

and kids' cots and highchairs too.

☎ 9250 9555 🖥 www .savillesuites.com ✉ 2 Bond St 🚇 Wynyard, Circular Quay 🚌 ⛴ Circular Quay 🅿 ♿ fair 🍴 bar, restaurant 🚭

Stellar Suites (5, E8) If you're staying in Sydney for a while, this is a good place to set up shop. Close to Hyde Park, city and Oxford St, self-contained suites are spacious and functional with kitchenette, data ports and friendly reception for 24-hour smiles.

☎ 9264 9754 🖥 www .stellarsuites.com ✉ 4 Wentworth Ave 🚇 Museum 🅿 ♿ fair 🍴 café 🚭

About Sydney

HISTORY

Australia can seem to be a long way from anywhere in particular, an isolation that made it the last great landmass to be 'discovered' by Europeans. But before Sydney Harbour saw its first billow of British sail, indigenous people inhabited the continent for more than 40,000 years, the world's longest continuous cultural history.

Aboriginal Origins

When the British first sailed into Warran (the Aboriginal name for Sydney Harbour) there were an estimated 3000 Aborigines living in the area, and around one million across the continent. The Sydney region is the ancestral home of the Eora people (the Ku-ring-gai, Birrabirragul and Cadi tribes) who possessed an intimate understanding of environmental sustainability, spoke three distinct languages and maintained sophisticated sacred and artistic cultures.

Old and new pursuits: Bondi rock engravings

Under colonial rule, Aborigines were stripped of all legal rights to their land. In a typically ugly pattern of European colonisation, they were systematically incarcerated, killed or driven away by force – thousands more succumbed to European diseases.

A legacy of 2000 Aboriginal rock engravings exists in the Sydney area, and many Sydney suburbs have Aboriginal names.

European Settlement

Portuguese navigators bumped into Australia in the 16th century, followed shortly by Dutch explorers and the enterprising Englishman (read: pirate) William Dampier. British hunger for new world territories landed Captain James Cook on the east coast in 1770. Cook claimed the continent for England and, in a fit of creative genius, named it New South Wales (NSW).

Bennelong

The volatile, puzzled relations between Bennelong, an Eora Aborigine, and the British are emblematic of much early contact.

In 1789 Governor Phillip kidnapped Bennelong to act as an interpreter and go-between. He initially enjoyed life at Government House, but the following years became a confused parade of escape, recapture, anger and misunderstanding. Bennelong travelled with Phillip to England, returning to Australia after two uncomfortable years and retreating from white contact.

Bennelong Point, where a house was built for him and where the Sydney Opera House now stands, bears his name.

Sailing home, Joseph Banks (Cook's naturalist) suggested relieving Britain's overcrowded prisons by transporting convicts to the new colony. The British government sparked at the concept – faraway convicts were good convicts.

In 1787 the First Fleet set sail from Portsmouth with 759 convicts aboard. At the helm was Captain Arthur Phillip, deigned to become first governor of NSW. Phillip made landfall at Botany Bay on 26 January 1788 before shunting north to Sydney Cove. He flirted with the name 'Albion' but astutely opted for Sydney (the British Home Secretary, Baron Sydney of Chislehurst, was responsible for the colonies at the time).

Captain Phillip keeps an eye on the town

Colonial Expansion

In 1800 there were only three small settlements in the colony – Sydney Cove, Parramatta, and on Norfolk Island, adrift in the Pacific 1500km east of Sydney. The continent's vast interior was largely unknown. Over the next 40 years, Sydney bumbled through near-starvation and rum-fuelled political turmoil, while exploration opened up western NSW to settlers. Sydney town grew steadily, with convict transportation continuing until 1840. Free settlers arrived, too, but things didn't boom until the 1850s gold rush put a rocket under the economy. Hefty discoveries near Bathurst and in Victoria had prospectors flooding in from Europe, Asia and North America. Sydney's population doubled in a decade.

The 20th Century

On 1 January 1901, NSW became a state of the new Australian nation.

Through WWI and the Great Depression, Australia remained culturally and economically tied to Britain, but after the US defended Australia from the Japanese in WWII, a fraternal shift towards America occurred.

Post-war immigrants from the UK, Ireland and the Mediterranean brought spirit and prosperity to Australia in the 1950s and '60s and Sydney's urban area spread like spilt honey.

The face of Sydney changed again during the Vietnam War, when American GIs swarmed to the city on 'rest and recreation'. Kings Cross excelled in providing the kind of belt-level R and R that the troops lusted for.

The bullish world economy of the 1980s sprouted a forest of bombastic new Sydney skyscrapers, with 1988's controversial celebration of the bicentenary of British landing ruffling indigenous and pro-republican feathers.

Sydney Today

Hosting the 2000 Olympic Games thrust Sydney into the global limelight, and the city wasn't shy about stepping onto the stage. The coup of securing the Olympics gripped the city in a late-'90s sweat of building activity, the flawless success of the Games infusing confidence and pride. An expansive metropolis of four million folks, Sydney's streets buzz with business conducted in dozens of accents and tongues. Confidence remains, but there's a sense of post-Olympic reflection and cultural re-definition in the air. The ebullient '80s are ancient history and Sydney has surfed the Olympic wave right into the beach – everyone's catching their breath and waiting to see what'll happen next.

A Whale Of A Time

After an extended absence due to apocalyptic commercial whaling in the 19th century, whales have made a return to Sydney Harbour. A traditional detour for humpback and southern right whales migrating south for the summer, the harbour has hosted pods of whales breaching below the Harbour Bridge in each of the past three years. If you're lucky enough to be out on the water with them, give them a wide berth – they're bigger than you are, and humanity owes them a little peace and quiet.

ENVIRONMENT

Sydney and its stupendous harbour are encircled by parks and forests. Beauty comes naturally, as does the incentive to keep things looking good. Locals generate as much mess as anyone else, but they're also environmentally aware.

Sydney's Gods of Rain don't pull any punches, with summer downpours sending people scurrying. Historically, Sydney's harbour and beaches gasped and clogged after heavy rains, but million-dollar litter traps now prevent a lot of rubbish flowing into the harbour. Still, swimming at harbour beaches such as Balmoral or Seven Shillings after a big storm can be a soupy experience.

Shark Beach at Vaucluse – don't worry, there's a tooth-proof net

Airport noise creates headaches under the flight path – the government has tried to calm nervy, under-slept locals by spreading aircraft trajectories.

The air in the city and eastern suburbs is generally clean and breezy; the west can be wheezy.

GOVERNMENT & POLITICS

Sydney is the capital of NSW and seat of state government, which holds court in Parliament House on Macquarie St.

NSW has two main political parties: the left-wing Australian Labor Party and right-wing Liberal/National party coalition. At research time, Labor held government with Premier Bob Carr on top of the heap. Members of the Australian Greens, Australian Democrats and several independents also populate Parliament.

Sydneysiders can be wryly cynical about state politics. State elections irritate the public every four years and there's not a whole lotta love for Bob Carr's Labor machine that some people feel has abandoned traditional values to court big-business dollars. Your views on Australia's prospective move towards becoming a republic may see you lauded as a visionary, or tarred, feathered and banished to the Blue Mountains.

Don't expect much saucy media coverage of politicians' sex lives. Perhaps it's an aesthetic damnation, but locals don't drool over Clinton-Lewinsky/Tory-sex-romp scandals. A contraceptive distance is maintained between the media and politicians.

How Much?	
The *Sydney Morning Herald*	$1.20
Schooner of beer about	$3.60
One hour's car parking	$3–10
Litre of unleaded petrol about	$1
Harbour Bridge road toll	$3
Local call on a public phone	$0.40
Disposable camera	$20
Stamp for a local letter	$0.50

We'll cross that bridge when we come to it

ECONOMY

Sydney is Australia's chief commercial, financial and industrial centre, whipping up a quarter of Australia's economic activity. The city's economic growth rate routinely tops the national average, nudging over 5% in recent years. As a financial centre, Sydney houses 'the big three' – the Reserve Bank of Australia, Australian Stock Exchange and Sydney Futures Exchange – and most of Australia's major banks have their head offices in Sydney. It's also a transport epicentre, with two harbours – Port Jackson (Sydney Harbour) and Botany Bay – a hyperactive airport and a spider-web rail network. The majority of Australia's foreign trade flows through Sydney and NSW. The tourism sector is currently booming, with over four million local and international visitors to Sydney annually – expect Sydney to handle your arrival with aplomb!

SOCIETY, CULTURE & IDENTITY

Sydney is irresistibly multicultural, with a quarter of Sydneysiders born overseas. Before WWII Sydney was predominantly Anglo-Irish, but large post-war migrations from Italy, Greece, Yugoslavia, Lebanon and Turkey enriched the mix. The Chinese first arrived during the 1850s gold rush; Asian migration continuing with large numbers of Vietnamese after the Vietnam War. Other significant numbers have recently arrived from New Zealand, Thailand, Cambodia and the Philippines.

A waning majority of Australians are Christian. The Presbyterian, Methodist and Congregational Union churches merged to form the Uniting Church in 1977, although the Anglican Church remains separate. Australia's Irish and Mediterranean heritage keeps Roman Catholic pews warm. Non-Christian minorities abound – Islam is Australia's second-largest religion, Jewish numbers are steady, Buddhism is increasingly popular and 13% of Australians claim agnosticism, although a recent attempt was made to register 'Jedi' as an Australian creed.

> **Just the Facts Ma'am**
> - The annual number of overseas visitors to Sydney is over 2.3 million.
> - Over 55% of overseas visitors to Australia spend time in Sydney.
> - More than 40% of migrants to Australia settle in the Sydney area.
> - The average Sydneysider occupies six times more space than the average cramped Tokyo tenant.
> - Sydney's population is growing by 130 people a day.

Dude, get off the runway!

Aboriginal Society

Although non-indigenous Australia is at last recognising the complexities of Aboriginal culture, many are still intolerant of urban Aborigines. Aborigines comprise just 0.6% of Sydney's population, but they're marginalised and frequently cast as social miscreants. Misunderstandings are common, with constructive solutions to indigenous poverty, criminality and health problems placed in the 'too hard' basket. Inner-city Redfern has a large Koori (indigenous southeastern Australian) population, although the suburb's dilapidated heritage houses are fast being consumed by renovators and developers. See Lonely Planet's *Aboriginal Australia* guide for more detailed information on indigenous culture.

Etiquette

Sydney's pace is frenetic – attitudes can be aggressive and in-your-face, but locals are generally friendly and open-minded. Gay and lesbian Sydney is riotously uninhibited. Smokers beware: restaurants and sporting arenas are smoke-free. Mobile phone etiquette is forgiving – perhaps too forgiving. Turn yours off during meetings, movies and concerts.

Business conduct is straightforward – astute candour seals the deal; obsequious smooth-talking (a.k.a. 'brown-nosing') won't. Much business discussion happens after work at the pub – 'a couple of quieties' (a beer or two) often involves more than just a drink. Business dress is sharp with an allowance for individuality (and that you may have just been for a surf).

ARTS

Sun, sand, surf and sin are misleading folly – Sydney is no artistic backwater. It can't rival New York or London for artistic quantity, but Sydney breeds equally bold, adventurous, artistic attitudes. Opening nights, readings and screenings are firmly entrenched in the social calendar.

Well-hung: Art Gallery of NSW

Painting

Before the 1880s, Australian painters applied European aesthetics to Antipodean landscapes, failing to capture Australia's bleached light, ragged forests and earthy colours with any certainty. Melbourne's distinctly Australian Heidelberg School changed this in 1885. Tom Roberts and Arthur Streeton brought the Heidelberg stylings to Sydney in 1891.

Expressionists of the 1940s such as Sidney Nolan and Arthur Boyd blazed their way to prominence and rattled the national psyche. Sydney's Brett Whiteley (1939–92) was an internationally notorious *enfant terrible* who let loose with luscious, colourful, orgasmic canvases. His Surry Hills studio is preserved as a gallery (p29).

Aboriginal Art

Art is integral to Aboriginal culture, a conduit between past and present, supernatural and earthly, people and land. Aboriginal art is immersed in 'The Dreaming' – a vast unchanging network of life and land tracing back to spiritual ancestors of the Dreamtime.

Aboriginal art gained broad cross-cultural exposure in the 1980s and '90s when galleries discovered its virtue and value. Dot paintings are exquisite, as are Tiwi Island woodcarvings and fabrics, Arnhem Land bark paintings and central Australian prints. Many galleries specialise in Aboriginal and Torres Strait Islander art (p31).

Literature

Like Australian painters, local writers (Henry Lawson, AB 'Banjo' Patterson and Miles Franklin) spiked a vernacular vein in the late 1800s. Modern Australian authors like Patrick White (Nobel Prize 1973), Tom Keneally (Booker Prize 1982), Peter Carey (Booker Prize 1988 and 2001) and Tim

Sydney Structures

Sydney is predominantly a Victorian city, with much of the city's expensive inner-city housing stock dating from this era. Colonial structures to have survived Sydney's wholesale 20th-century development are scarce, but remnants are culturally celebrated. Classy Art Deco design reigned between the two world wars, most obviously (and perhaps incongruously) finding an outlet in Sydney pub architecture. Some unbelievable eyesores sprouted with the lifting of the 150ft building height limit in the late 1950s, many architects accused of lazily dominating Sydney's splendorous natural setting rather than designing anything of objective or complementary beauty. Utzon's Sydney Opera House stands as a beacon of architectural delight as the CBD continues its rise.

Winton have redefined what being Australian is. Robert Drewe, Helen Garner, David Malouf, Kate Grenville, Janette Turner Hospital, Thea Astley, Murray Bail, Elizabeth Jolley, Eleanor Dark and Richard Flanagan are all worthy reads.

At the pinnacle of Australian poetry are Gwen Harwood, Les Murray, Francis Webb, Peter Porter, Judith Wright, Faye Zwicky, Bruce Dawe, Anthony Lawrence, Kevin Hart, Oodgeroo Noonuccal and Jack Davis.

See www.austlit.edu.au for more info, p80 for **Sydney Writers' Festival** details and p55 for Sydney-centric reads.

Opera House operatics

Music

Sydney's sounds: world-class opera, grungy pub bands, funky electronic acts. Local musos gig at pubs and clubs around the city, while international acts rock big venues like the Sydney Entertainment Centre (p85) and the Enmore Theatre (p84).

Sydney's raucous rock scene (the Easybeats, Midnight Oil, Silverchair etc) ailed under '90s noise and licensing restrictions, but is making a comeback. There's an effervescent dance-music scene, with clubs and dance parties catering to every sub-genre. Jazz and blues are kickin' in venues like The Basement and Soup Plus (jazz) and pubs like the Empire and Annandale (blues). See p84 for more.

Opera Australia wails through 18 operas a year, based (appropriately) at the Opera House. The Sydney Symphony, Australia's biggest orchestra, plays 140 concerts annually, frequently at the Opera House and City Recital Hall.

January's **Sydney Festival** (see p91) tunes Sydney's diverse musical movements. The **Sydney Discography** boxed text lists some sound Sydney sounds; see p84.

Backstreet guitar shop – Kings Cross rocks

Film

Sydney's film industry is booming. 1990's efforts such as *Strictly Ballroom*, *Shine*, *Muriel's Wedding* and *Priscilla – Queen of the Desert* consolidated Sydney's reputation as a top-shelf production location, while local actors such as Russell Crowe, Nicole Kidman, Naomi Watts, Cate Blanchett and Geoffrey Rush rode the Hollywood fame train.

Sydney's multimillion dollar Fox Studios (2, D5) rolls out big-budget world extravaganzas including *The Matrix* trilogy, *Mission Impossible 2*, the *Star Wars* prequels and Sydneysider Baz Luhrmann's *Moulin Rouge*.

Sydney has two international film festivals: see p80 for Bondi's **Flickerfest** details and p87 for **Tropfest** info.

Dance

Dance and Sydney's body-focused audiences go hand-in-hand (and

> ## Sydney on the Silver Screen
> Sydney sure is a good-lookin' sheila (see Language, p122), a fact not overlooked in these Sydney movies:
> - *Lantana* (2001; director Ray Lawrence) Mystery for grown-ups meditating on love, truth and grief.
> - *Looking for Alibrandi* (2000; director Kate Woods) Growing up Italian in Sydney suburbia.
> - *Puberty Blues* (1981; director Bruce Beresford) South Sydney's '70s surf culture at its most 'perf'.
> - *Two Hands* (1999; director Gregor Jordan) Vicious humour in Sydney's criminal underworld.
> - *Finding Nemo* (2003; director Andrew Stanton) Animated kids' classic using many local voices including Barry Humphries as Bitin' Bruce, a shark member of Carnivores Anonymous.

cheek-to-cheek). Australian dancers have a fearless reputation for awesome physical displays (and sometimes a lack of costume). The talented Australian Ballet troupe tours a mixed programme of classical and modern ballets, frocking-up four times a year at the Sydney Opera House (p12).

Graeme Murphy's Sydney Dance Company (p90) leads Australia in contemporary dance. The acclaimed Bangarra Dance Theatre (p89) conjures up an incendiary blend of 40,000 years of indigenous performance tradition and vigorous new choreography.

Indigenous performance – a highlight of any Sydney visit (p89)

Directory

'Let's sell ice cream at Bondi in July.' Great idea Barry...

ARRIVAL & DEPARTURE

Air

Sydney's major airport is **Kingsford Smith** (1, E3), 10km south of the city centre. The international and domestic terminals are a 4km, $4 bus or train ride apart. Getting to the city from Kingsford Smith (or vice versa) is easiest by train or car. To confirm arrival/departure times call airlines directly or log on to the airport website's 'Flight Finder'.

INFORMATION

General Inquiries ☎ 9667 9111; www.sydneyairport.com.au

Lost Property ☎ 9667 9583

Qantas Flight Information ☎ 13 12 23; www.qantas.com.au

Virgin Flight Information ☎ 13 67 89; www.virginblue.com.au

Carpark Information ☎ 9667 6010

AIRPORT ACCESS
Bus

Bookings are essential for both services.

Kingsford Smith Transport/ Airporter (☎ 9666 9988; single/ return $8/13; ✹ 24hr) Connects the airport and central Sydney hotels.

Manly Airport Bus (☎ 0500 505 800; single/return $28/56) Runs a door-to-door service to/from Manly.

Taxi

A ride to or from Circular Quay should cost $25 to $35; to/from Central Station $20 to $25.

Train

Airport Link (☎ 13 15 00; www .airportlink.com.au; single/return from Central Station to domestic terminal $11/16.10, to international terminal $11.60/17.30; ✹ every 10min 5.10am-11.45pm Mon-Fri, 5.15-12.15am Sat & Sun) Runs from city train stations. Return fares are cheaper after 9am and on weekends. A one-way trip takes about 15min.

LEFT LUGGAGE

Large lockers are available in the domestic and international arrivals halls. Oversize items can only be stored in the international lockers.

Bus

Interstate and regional bus travellers arrive at **Sydney Coach Terminal** (5, D9; ☎ 9281 9366; Eddy Ave; ✹ 6am-10.30pm) outside Central Station. Major bus companies have offices nearby. Luggage lockers are available at **Bay 14** ($7-12; ✹ 24hr).

Train

Sydney's main rail terminus for Countrylink interstate and regional services is **Central Station** (5, D9; ☎ 13 22 32; Eddy Ave; ✹ staffed ticket booths 6am-9.30pm, ticket machines 24hr). Call for information, arrival and departure times, and to make reservations. Luggage lockers are also available here ($4-8/24hr).

Travel Documents
PASSPORT

Passports are required for all overseas visitors and must be valid for at least six months from date of entry.

VISA

Visas are required for all overseas visitors except New Zealand nationals who sheepishly receive a 'special category' visa on arrival. Visa application forms are available from diplomatic missions, travel agents and the Department of Immigration and Multicultural and Indigenous Affairs (☎ 13 18 81; www.immi.gov.au).

RETURN/ONWARD TICKET
Onward tickets aren't compulsory, but immigration officials may grill you if you don't have one.

Customs & Duty Free
Amounts of more than A$10,000 cash and goods of animal or vegetable origin must be declared at customs. Don't even *think* about bringing in or leaving with flora, fauna or drugs – **Australian Customs** (☎ 1300 363 263; www .customs.gov.au) doesn't tolerate smugglers. Sydney airport has two customs channels: green (nothing to declare) and red (something to declare).

Travellers over 18 years may import 1125mL of liquor, 250 cigarettes or 250g of tobacco and dutiable goods up to the value of A$400 per person (A$200 for under 18s).

Australia has a 10% Goods and Services Tax (GST) automatically applied to most purchases, though some food items are exempt. If you purchase goods with a total minimum value of $300 from any one supplier within 30 days of departure from Australia, you're entitled to a GST refund. You can get a cheque refund at the designated booth located past Customs at Sydney Airport or contact Australian Customs: Tourist Refund Scheme.

GETTING AROUND

Trains, buses and ferries run by the State Transit Authority of NSW (STA; ☎ 13 15 00; www.131500 .com.au) are generally convenient, reliable and good value. Contact them for information or visit their Circular Quay information booths. Beware: fare-dodgers receive a $100 on-the-spot fine.

In this book, the nearest train/Monorail/MLR/ferry station or bus route is noted after the 🚆 Ⓜ 🚉 🚊 or 🚌 icon in each listing.

Travel Passes
SydneyPass (www.sydneypass.info; 3/5/7 days $90/120/140) Offers bus, rail and ferry transport, travel on the Sydney and Bondi Explorer buses, harbour ferry cruises and a return trip on the Airport Express train. They're available from the **Sydney Visitor Centre** (5, D3; ☎ 9240 8788; www .sydneyvisitorcentre.com; 106 George St, The Rocks; ☉ 9am-6pm), the Circular Quay Bus Information Kiosk, at airport Visitor Information desks or by phoning ☎ 13 15 00.
DayTripper (☎ 13 15 00; www. cityrail.info; $15) STA day pass letting you ride most trains, buses and ferries with discounts at an array of attractions.

Bus
Buses run almost everywhere, but they are slower than trains. Bondi Beach, Coogee and parts of the North Shore are only serviced by bus. Nightrider buses operate skeletally after regular buses and trains cease around midnight.

Sydney is divided into seven zones, the city centre being 'Zone 1'. The main city bus stops are Circular Quay (5, D4), Wynyard Park on York St (5, C5) and Railway Square (5, C9).

Buy tickets from newsagencies, kiosks and buses (having the correct change helps to prevent bus driver wrath). Fares start at $1.60, with most trips being under $3.50.

There's a **Bus Information Kiosk** on the Alfred/Loftus St corner in Circular Quay (5, D4; 🕑 7am-7pm Mon-Fri, 8.30am-5pm Sat & Sun), near Wynyard station on Carrington St (5, C5) and outside the Queen Victoria Building on York St (5, C7). Bus routes starting with an X indicate limited-stop express routes; those with an L have limited stops. Bus routes listed in this book depart from Circular Quay unless otherwise indicated.

SPECIAL SERVICES
Sydney Explorer (STA; ☎ 13 15 00; www.sydneypass.info; $30/15 from driver & Bus Information Kiosks; 🕑 every 20min 8.40am-5.20pm) The red Sydney Explorer bus follows a two-hour, 22-stop hop-on, hop-off loop from Circular Quay through Kings Cross, Chinatown, Darling Harbour and The Rocks. The Sydney Explorer includes pithy on-board commentary and discounted entry to attractions.
Bondi Explorer (STA; ☎ 13 15 00; www.sydneypass.info; $30/15 from driver & Bus Information Kiosks; 🕑 every 30min 9.15am-4.15pm) The blue Bondi Explorer bus does a two-hour, 19-stop loop of the inner city and Eastern Suburbs, including Paddington, Double Bay, Vaucluse, Watsons Bay and Bondi Beach.
CitySightseeing Sydney Tour (☎ 9567 8400; www.city-sightseeing.com) A privately run rival/alternative to the Explorer buses, with parallel services and prices.

USEFUL BUS ROUTES FROM CIRCULAR QUAY

Balmain	431-4, 441-2, 445-6
Bondi Beach	380, 389 or L82 from Circular Quay, 381-2 from Bondi Junction
Coogee	372-4, X73-4, 313-4 & 353 from Bondi Junction
Darling Harbour	443, 456
Glebe	431-4
Kings Cross	323-7, 324-5, 333
Leichhardt	370, 413, 436-40, 446
Manly	151, 169, E69 from Wynyard Park
Maroubra	376-7, 395-6, X77, X96
Newtown	355, 370, 422-3, 426, 428
Paddington	352, 378, 380, 389, L82
Surry Hills	301-04, 375, 390-1
Watsons Bay	324-5, L24, L82 from Bondi Junction

Train
CITYRAIL
Sydney's trains are the deft way to get around town. Trains run from around 5am to midnight. Twenty-four-hour ticket machines occupy most stations but humans are usually available too if you'd rather talk to something that'll listen. There's a **CityRail Information Booth** (5, D4; ☎ 13 15 00; www.131500.com.au; 🕑 9.05am-4.50pm) behind Wharf 5 at Circular Quay.

MONORAIL
The **Metro Monorail** (☎ 9285 5600; www.metromonorail.com.au; circuit $4, day pass $8; 🕑 every 4min 7am-10pm Mon-Thu, to midnight Fri & Sat, 8am-10pm Sun) circles like a lugubrious elevated worm between Darling Harbour and the city.

METRO LIGHT RAIL (MLR)
The future-slick **MLR** (☎ 9285 5600; www.metrolightrail.com.au; single $2.60-4.90, day pass $8; 🕑 24hr, every 15min 6am-midnight, every

30min midnight-6am) glides between Central Station and Pyrmont via Chinatown and Darling Harbour. The service beyond Pyrmont to Lilyfield stops at 11pm Sunday to Thursday, midnight Friday and Saturday. MLR stops are marked in this book with the 🚈 icon.

Boat

Sydney transport's most civilised option – harbour ferries, JetCats (to Manly) and RiverCats (to Parramatta) – depart from Circular Quay. The STA's **Ferry Information Office** (☎ 9207 3170; www.sydneyferries. info; single $4-7; ⏱ 7am-5.45pm Mon-Sat, 8am-5.45pm Sun) has details. Many ferries have connecting bus services.

WATER TAXI
Yellow Water Taxis (☎ 9299 1099; www.yellowwatertaxis.com.au; adult/child $12.50/7.50; ⏱ 7am-midnight) shuttle between Circular Quay and Darling Harbour and run 40min harbour tours ($25/15). Rides to/from other harbour venues can be booked.

Taxi

Taxis can be flagged down when their top-light is aglow. There are patrolled Friday/Saturday-night taxi ranks at the Four Seasons Hotel (5, D4), the Wentworth Hotel (5, D5) and on Park St between George and Pitt Sts (5, D7). Other ranks are at Central, Wynyard and Circular Quay stations. The four major taxi companies offer phone bookings:

Legion	☎ 13 14 51
Premier Cabs	☎ 13 10 17
RSL Cabs	☎ 13 22 11
Taxis Combined	☎ 8332 8888

FARES & CHARGES
Flag fall is $2.65 then it's $1.53/km (+20% 10pm-6am). The waiting charge is 67¢/min; the 10¢/kg charge for luggage over 25kg is often waived. Passengers must pay bridge, tunnel and road tolls (even if you don't incur them 'outbound', the returning driver will incur them 'inbound'). There's a $1.10 phone-booking fee.

APPROXIMATE FARES
City-Newtown	💲	12
City-Bondi Beach	💲	25
City-Airport	💲	30

Car & Motorcycle

Masochistic? Bring your car into central Sydney. The city has a confusing spaghetti-like one-way street system, parking is hell, parking inspectors are ruthless demons (also from hell) and tow-away zones prevail. Private car parks are expensive – around $15 per hour. Venues in the book where on-site parking is available are marked with the 🅿 icon.

A car is, however, invaluable for exploring outer Sydney. Many hotels include parking in accommodation packages. Red-light and speed cameras are common – rental companies will send you your fines plus hefty 'processing' fees.

ROAD RULES
If you want to stay in one piece, drive on the left-hand side of the road and wear your seat belt (front and back seat). Cyclists (motor and pedal) must sacrifice style for helmets. The minimum driving age is 18. The speed limit is 60km/h (50km/h in built-up areas) and 100km/h to 110km/h on motorways. The blood-alcohol limit is 0.05% and its enforced with random breath checks – loss of licence and hefty fines await the infringer.

There's a $3 southbound toll on the Sydney Harbour Bridge and Tunnel; $4 northbound on the

Eastern Distributor. Sydney's main motorways are also tolled.

RENTAL
Expect to pay about $70 per day for a zippy small car. Petrol costs about $1 per litre. The following stalwarts have airport and city offices:

Avis	☎ 13 63 33
Budget	☎ 13 27 27
Hertz	☎ 13 30 39,
(international)	1800 550 067
Thrifty	☎ 1300 367 227

DRIVING LICENCE & PERMITS
Visitors can drive using their home-country driving licence for three months.

MOTORING ORGANISATIONS
The **National Roads & Motorists Association** (NRMA; 5, D6; ☎ 13 21 32; 74-76 King St) has reciprocal arrangements with similar motoring organisations overseas and can provide you with 24-hour emergency roadside assistance (☎ 13 11 11) and travel, insurance and accommodation advice.

PRACTICALITIES

Climate & When to Go
It is comfortable to visit Sydney at any time of the year. Temperatures rarely fall below 10°C in winter while summer maximums hover around 25°C (77°F). Breathlessly humid summer days occasionally hit 40°C (104°F), but the sea breeze usually kicks in and stops people blowing their cool. Autumn's clear warm days and mild nights ply the spirit with easy delight. There's more chance of rain during spring, but showers usually clear up pretty quickly. From October to March humidity is high, but torrential downpours often help break the heat.

January is the school-holiday peak season. Other school holidays fall around Easter, late June to mid-July and late September to early October.

Consulates
Most foreign embassies are based in Canberra, but many countries have a Sydney consulate, including:

Japan (5, D5; ☎ 9231 3455; 52 Martin Pl)
New Zealand (5, D5; ☎ 8256 2000; 55 Hunter St)
UK (5, D4; ☎ 9247 7521; 1 Macquarie Pl)
USA (5, D5; ☎ 9373 9200; 19-29 Martin Pl)

Disabled Travellers
WHEELCHAIR ACCESS
Most of Sydney's attractions are accessible to wheelchair travellers. All new or renovated venues cater for wheelchairs but older buildings are harder to access. Most of the National Trust's historic houses are at least partially accessible – embarrassed attendants can usually show you photos of inaccessible areas.

Taxis can usually accommodate wheelchairs – advise the operator when making a booking. Wheelchair-friendly listings in this book are marked with the ♿ icon and

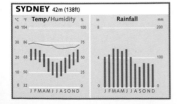

rated from 'fair' to 'excellent', fair indicating minimal accessibility.

HEARING LOOPS
Most of Sydney's major attractions offer hearing loops and sign language interpreters for hearing-impaired travellers. Check in advance in all cases.

PARKING
Sydney has a proliferation of parking spaces reserved for disabled drivers. International travellers should contact the **Roads and Traffic Authority** (☎ 13 22 13; www.rta.nsw.gov.au) if a temporary parking permit is needed.

INFORMATION & ORGANISATIONS
The **City of Sydney website** (www.cityofsydney.nsw.gov.au) lists venues with good wheelchair access. Also check:

Deaf Society of NSW (☎ 9893 8555/8858; L4, 169 Macquarie St, Parramatta, 2150)
NICAN (☎ 6285 3713, 1800 806 769; Box 407 Curtin, ACT 2605)
Royal Blind Society of NSW (☎ 9334 3333, 4 Mitchell St, Enfield, 2136)

USEFUL PUBLICATIONS
Useful references include *Access Sydney* (Spinal Cord Injuries Australia; www.spinalcordinjuries.com.au) and *Access for All* (National Parks and Wildlife Service; ☎ 1300 361 967).

Discounts
Many attractions offer child/family/student/senior discounts. Concession prices listed in this book apply for full-time students and seniors.

The **See Sydney & Beyond Card** (www.seesydneycard.com; 1/2/3/7 days with transport $75/130/175/250, without $59/99/129/189) offers admission to a wide range of Sydney's attractions including sight-seeing tours, harbour cruises, museums, historic buildings and wildlife parks, with or without public transport included. It is available at the Sydney Visitor Centre (see p122).

The Historic Houses Trust's **Ticket Through Time** admits you to all 11 of the HHT's houses and museums. See p28 for more information.

STUDENT & YOUTH CARDS
Most tourist attractions recognise the **International Student Identity Card** (ISIC), not valid for public transport concessions.

SENIORS' CARDS
Some places may agree to a discount via Seniors Cards from other countries, although most seniors' discounts are restricted to Australian citizens.

Electricity
Bring adaptors for US flat two-pin plugs and European round two-pin plugs, or purchase them from travel-goods shops, hardware shops and chemists.

Voltage	220-240V AC
Frequency	50Hz
Plugs	flat three-pin

Emergencies
Sydney isn't a dangerous city, but be sure to use big-city common sense. Kings Cross can be brawly and bawdy, while Redfern and some of the back streets of Glebe closest to the city can be dodgy. Australian pickpockets aren't highly evolved artists, but don't be complacent in touristy areas. Police stations are in every suburb – contact them locally.

Ambulance	☎ 000
Fire	☎ 000
Police	☎ 000
Lifeline	☎ 13 11 14
Rape Crisis Centre	☎ 9819 6565

Fitness

Sydney's sunshine, parks and un-ashamed vanity provide plenty of impetus to get your pulse pumping and your bod buffed.

CYCLING

With steep hills, narrow streets and traffic, Sydney isn't exactly a bike-friendly place, although some roads do have designated cycle lanes.

Bicycle NSW (☎ 9281 4099; www .bicyclensw.org.au) Publishes Cycling Around Sydney showing city routes and paths. Centennial Park is popular for pedalling, with less traffic and long paths.

Woolys Wheels (6, C4; ☎ 9331 2671; www.woolyswheels.com; 82 Oxford St, Paddington; $33/day; ☯ 9am-6pm Mon-Fri, to 8pm Thu, to 4pm Sat, 11am-4pm Sun) Rents out quality bikes on Centennial Park's doorstep.

GOLF

There are 80-plus courses in the metropolitan area, though half are private. Book to play on public courses (especially on weekends) or swing some nepotism to chip onto private greens.

Moore Park Golf Course (2, C5; ☎ 9663 1064; www.mooreparkgolf.com .au; cnr Anzac Pde & Cleveland Sts; Mon-Fri $35, Sat & Sun $40; ☯ 6am-10pm) The CBD's closest public course (18-hole, par 70). Golf lessons $50/30min.

Bondi Beach Golf Club (3, C1; ☎ 9130 1981; www.bondigolf.com; 5 Military Rd, North Bondi; full day $18.50, after 4pm $11; ☯ 7am-8pm) Spectacular cliff-top public course (9-hole, par 28).

GYMS

Most large hotels have a gym and swimming pool for guests; many make these facilities available to visitors for a fee. Otherwise, there's an abundance of independent gyms around town.

City Gym (6, A3; ☎ 9360 6247; www .citygym.com.au; 107 Crown St, East Sydney; casual visit $13.50; ☯ 24hr) Weights, sauna, yoga, aerobics and massage (everything your body missed on the flight over).

JOGGING

The foreshore from Circular Quay to Woolloomooloo – through the Royal Botanic Gardens to The Domain – is well trodden. Centennial Park, Bondi and Manly beach promenades and the Bondi to Bronte clifftop trail (p39) are also popular. You might see strange blue stripes on some Sydney roads. This is the route the marathon runners followed in the 2000 Olympics, but jogging along it is not advised.

SAILING & BOATING

Sydney's sailing schools are many; a sailing lesson is a superb way to see the harbour. The **Cruising Yacht Club of Australia** (☎ 9363 9731; www.cyca.com.au) fields general inquiries. **EastSail Sailing School** (p46) runs lessons for all levels of seaworthiness.

SURFING

South Shore: get tubed in the green room at Bondi, Tamarama, Coogee, Maroubra and Cronulla. North Shore: there are a dozen gnarly surf beaches between Manly and Palm Beach. Surfboards, boogie-boards and wetsuits can be hired from seaside shops.

For lessons in how to carve up the swell, see Bondi's **Let's Go Surfing** and **Manly Surf School** (p34). Radical dude.

SWIMMING

Harbour beaches offer sheltered and shark-netted swimming, but nothing beats (or cures a hangover faster than) Pacific Ocean waves. There are 100+ public swimming pools in Sydney and many beaches have protected rock pools (see p35).

Andrew 'Boy' Charlton Pool (2, C4; ☎ 9358 6686; www.abcpool.org; 1C Mrs Macquaries Rd, The Domain; $5; ⊙ 6.30am-8pm Oct-Apr) A 50m outdoor saltwater pool named after the 1924 Olympian; five-star amenities and harbour-view café.

Cook & Phillip Park Aquatic & Fitness Centre (6, A2; ☎ 9326 0444; www.cookandphillip.com.au; 4 College St; pool $5.50, gym & pool $16; ⊙ 6am-10pm Mon-Fri, 7am-8pm Sat & Sun) Has three pools, gym, basketball court, carpark and café.

TENNIS

There are hundreds of public tennis courts in Sydney. **Tennis NSW** (☎ 9763 7644; www.tennisnsw.com .au) provides information.

Millers Point Tennis Court (5, C4; ☎ 9256 2222 or book at Observatory Hotel; Kent St, The Rocks; $25/hr; ⊙ 8am-10.30pm) Hard court cut into a classically Sydney leafy sandstone nook.

Parklands Tennis Centre (2, D5; ☎ 9662 7521; www.parklands.city-search.com.au; cnr Anzac & Lang Rds, Moore Park; $22/hr, $16/hr before 5pm Mon-Fri; ⊙ 9am-10pm Mon-Fri, to 8pm Fri, 8am-7pm Sat & Sun) Has synthetic-grass and hard courts.

YOGA

Yoga is so popular you'd think all of Sydney was looking through its third eye. Bondi Junction is yoga central, with around 10 schools. The following teach both Hatha and Ashtanga yoga:

Yoga Synergy (2, D5; ☎ 9389 7399; www.yogasynergy.com; L1, 115 Bronte Rd; casual class $16/14; ⊙ 6am-8pm) Also at 196 Australia St, Newtown.

Yogamat (2, D5; ☎ 9386 5284; www .yogamat.com.au; Suite 3, 354 Oxford St, entry from Vernon St; casual class $16; ⊙ 6am-8.45pm)

Gay & Lesbian Travellers

Gay and lesbian culture is almost mainstream in Sydney. Oxford St around **Taylor Sq** (5, F9) is the centre of arguably the second-largest gay community in the world. Some local gays think Taylor Sq has become something of a touristy gay ghetto and have migrated to areas of Kings Cross instead. Newtown is home to the city's lesbian scene.

Despite broad acceptance, there is still a homophobic streak among some community sections and violence against homosexuals is not unknown.

In NSW it's legal for men to have sex with men over 18, and for women to have sex with women over 16.

INFORMATION & ORGANISATIONS

Two free papers, *Capital Q Weekly* and *Sydney Star Observer* as well as *Lesbians on the Loose (LOTL)* have extensive listings. For counselling and referral call the **Gay & Lesbian Line** (☎ 9207 2800).

Health
IMMUNISATIONS

Immunisations are mandatory only if you're coming from a yellow fever–infected country (visit www .who.int/wer/ for a list); you'll need proof of vaccination.

PRECAUTIONS

Australia has the world's highest incidence of skin cancer, so cover up and slap on sunscreen. The sun is wickedest between 10am and 4pm –

dehydration and heat exhaustion are common. Take time to acclimatise and drink plenty of liquid (no, not beer). Tap water is drinkable.

Don't swim if you've been boozing and wait an hour after you've eaten. If you're struggling in the water, raise your arm and keep it raised until help arrives. Harbour beaches can be lousy for swimming after it rains – check radio and newspapers for updates on conditions.

Shark attacks are utterly rare, but if a siren sounds while you're swimming make for land pronto. Don't touch, eat or fool around with poisonous marine or land animals such as blue-ringed octopi and snakes. Sydney is also home to the notorious Sydney funnel-web spider – see p47.

Visit www.lonelyplanet.com or www.mdtravelhealth.com for further travel-health advice.

MEDICAL SERVICES
Australia has high-quality health care that isn't overly expensive by international standards, but travel insurance is essential to cover any medical treatment you may require. Visitors from Finland, Italy, Ireland, Malta, the Netherlands, New Zealand, Sweden and the UK have reciprocal health rights and can register at any **Medicare office** (☎ 13 20 11; www.health .gov.au/pubs/mbs/mbs3/medi care.htm). Hospitals with 24-hour accident and emergency departments include:

Royal North Shore Hospital (2, B2; ☎ 9926 7111; Pacific Hwy, St Leonards)
Royal Prince Alfred Hospital (2, B5; ☎ 9515 6111; Missenden Rd, Camperdown)
St Vincent's Hospital (6, B4; ☎ 8382 7111; cnr Victoria & Burton Sts, Darlinghurst)

Sydney Children's Hospital (2, D6; ☎ 9382 1111; High St, Randwick)
Sydney Hospital & Sydney Eye Hospital (5, E5; ☎ 9382 7111; 8 Macquarie St)

DENTAL SERVICES
If you chip a tooth or require emergency treatment, call the 24-hour information line ☎ 9369 7050 to be referred to the closest dentist.

PHARMACIES
Over-the-counter and prescribed medications are widely available at Sydney's privately run pharmacies. For urgent prescription requirements call the **Emergency Prescription Referral Service** (☎ 9966 8377). The following pharmacies have long opening hours:

Blake's Pharmacy (6, C2; ☎ 9358 6712; 28 Darlinghurst Rd, Kings Cross; ☉ 8am-midnight Mon-Sat, 9am-midnight Sun)
Darlinghurst Prescription Pharmacy (6, B4; ☎ 9361 5882; 261 Oxford St, Darlinghurst; ☉ 8am-10pm)
Park Pharmacy (2, B4; ☎ 9552 3372; 321 Glebe Point Rd, Glebe; ☉ 8am-8pm)
Wu's Pharmacy (5, C8; ☎ 9211 1805; 629 George St; ☉ 9am-9pm Mon-Sat, to 7pm Sun)

Holidays

Jan 1	New Year's Day
Jan 26	Australia Day
Late Mar/early Apr	Good Friday & Easter Monday
Apr 25	Anzac Day
June 10	Queen's Birthday
1st Mon in Aug	Bank Holiday
1st Mon in Oct	Labour Day
Dec 25	Christmas Day
Dec 26	Boxing Day

Internet

INTERNET SERVICE PROVIDERS

The local number for **CompuServe** is ☎ 9855 6940; for **AOL** ☎ 1300 734 357. Some local Internet service providers include:

OzEmail (☎ 13 28 84; www.ozemail .com.au)

Pacific Internet (☎ 8248 9500; www.pacific.net.au)

Telstra Big Pond (☎ 13 12 82; www.bigpond.com)

INTERNET CAFÉS

You can log on to the Internet at most public libraries, many hotels or Internet cafés throughout Sydney. Expect to pay $4 to $5 per hour.

Global Gossip (6, C3; ☎ 9326 9777; 111 Darlinghurst Rd, Kings Cross; per hr $4; ☻ 8am-midnight) A big conglomerate with most services, including scanning.

Internet World (5, D7; ☎ 9262 9700; 369 Pitt St; per hr $4; ☻ 24hr) Has fast servers and commercial FM beneath medicinal fluoro light.

Phone.Net.Cafe (3, B1; ☎ 9365 0681; 73 Hall St, Bondi; per hr $4; ☻ 8am-10pm) Has most services, toasted sandwiches, cakes and caffeine.

USEFUL WEBSITES

The **Lonely Planet website** at www .lonelyplanet.com offers speedy links to many of Sydney's websites. Others to try include:

Australian Tourist Commission (www.australia.com)

Bureau of Meteorology (www.bom .gov.au)

State Library of NSW (www.sl.nsw .gov.au)

Sydney City Council (www.sydneyof city.nsw.gov.au)

World City Guide (www.citysearch.com)

State Transit Authority (STA) (www.131500.com.au)

Surf Report (www.realsurf.com)

Lost Property

If you have lost something on public transport, call ☎ 9207 3166 (ferry), ☎ 9379 3341 (rail), ☎ 13 15 00 (bus) between 8am and 5pm Monday to Friday. It pays to make photocopies of your important documents, keep some with you (separate from the originals) and leave copies at home.

Metric System

Australia uses the metric system.

TEMPERATURE

$$°C = (°F - 32) ÷ 1.8$$
$$°F = (°C × 1.8) + 32$$

DISTANCE

1in = 2.54cm
1cm = 0.39in
1m = 3.3ft = 1.1yd
1ft = 0.3m
1km = 0.62 miles
1 mile = 1.6km

WEIGHT

1kg = 2.2lb
1lb = 0.45kg
1g = 0.04oz
1oz = 28g

VOLUME

1L = 0.26 US gallons
1 US gallon = 3.8L
1L = 0.22 imperial gallons
1 imperial gallon = 4.55L

Money

CURRENCY

The unit of currency is the Australian dollar, divided into 100 cents. When paying with cash, prices are rounded up or down to the nearest 5 cents. There are coins for $2, $1, 50¢, 20¢, 10¢ and 5¢, and notes for $100 (an 'avocado'), $50 ('pineapple'), $20 ('lobster'), $10 and $5.

TRAVELLERS CHEQUES

Travellers cheques are accepted in banks, large hotels and duty-free stores. **American Express** (☎ 9271 1111) and **Thomas Cook** (☎ 8585 7000) are widely recognised; they don't charge for cashing their own cheques and can usually arrange replacement cheques on-the-spot if yours go missing. Travellers cheques in Australian dollar can generally be exchanged at banks without paying commissions or fees.

CREDIT CARDS

American Express, Diners Club, MasterCard and Visa are all widely accepted credit cards. For lost cards contact:

American Express	☎ 1300 132 639
Diners Club	☎ 1300 360 060
MasterCard	☎ 1800 120 113
Visa	☎ 1800 450 346

ATMs

Twenty-four-hour automated teller machines (ATMs) accompany most bank branches, as well as some pubs and clubs. Banks usually accept debit cards linked to international network systems (Cirrus, Maestro, Barclays Connect, Solo etc) with a $1000 limit on daily withdrawals. Shops and retail outlets have **Eftpos** facilities for on-the-spot debit-card payments.

CHANGING MONEY

Foreign-exchange branches may offer marginally better exchange rates than the banks, and usually have longer opening hours and queue-free service. Check the rates, commissions and any other charges. All major newspapers list foreign exchange rates. Most licensed moneychangers are open retail hours and have branches near the Pitt St Mall, around Darling Harbour, Circular Quay and The Rocks.

Newspapers & Magazines

Daily newspapers are the tabloid *Daily Telegraph* and the broadsheets *Sydney Morning Herald*, the *Australian* and the *Australian Financial Review*.

Magazines with current affairs articles worth reading include the *Bulletin* and the Australian *Time*. Australia's *Rolling Stone* rocks.

Free street papers with local music and entertainment information include *Drum Media* (rock and alternative), *3D World* (club and dance), *Revolver*, *Sydney City Hub* and *Capital Q Weekly*.

Opening Hours

Banks, businesses and stores are closed on public holidays. Museums and other attractions often close on Christmas Day and Boxing Day.

Banks 9.30am-4pm Mon-Thu, 9.30am-5pm Fri; some large city branches 8am-6pm Mon-Thu, to 9pm Fri

Post Offices 9am-5pm Mon-Fri; some 10am-2pm Sat

Shops most open 9am-5.30pm Mon-Wed & Fri, to 9pm Thu, to 5pm Sat and 11am-5pm Sun

Pharmacies 8am-6pm (see p118)

Tourist Sites 9am-5pm (some closed Mon)

Photography & Video

Most tourist attractions are relaxed about people snapping photos and filming. The interiors of the Opera House theatres are subject to copyright, so photography and filming isn't allowed. Human clumsiness prohibits carrying a camera on the BridgeClimb over the Harbour Bridge.

Australia uses the PAL system, irritatingly incompatible with other video standards. Videos from the UK, New Zealand and many European, Asian and African countries are compatible; North American video is not.

Post

Sydney's **General Post Office** (GPO; 5, D5; ☎ 13 13 18; ⊙ 8.15am-5.30pm Mon-Fri, 10am-2pm Sat) is in the grandiose Victorian building on Martin Pl. A GPO counter service is around the corner at 130 Pitt St. Stamps are sold at post offices, Australia Post retail outlets and most newsagencies.

POSTAL RATES

Sending a postcard or standard letter within Australia costs 50¢; aerograms 85¢. Airmail postcards and letters (up to 50g) cost $1.10 to the Asia/Pacific region; $1.65 to the rest of the world. There's a nifty price guide at Australia Post's website (www.auspost.com.au).

Radio

2MBS (102.5FM) Subscriber-based music, arts and culture.
ABC Radio National (576AM) News and current affairs.
FBI (94.5FM) Sydney scene and 50% Australian musical content.
Triple J (105.7FM) Alternative youth rock and current affairs.

Telephone

Public payphones are either coin- or card-operated; local calls cost 40¢. Many also accept credit cards.

PHONECARDS

Local and international phonecards range in value from $5 to $50 – look for the phonecard logo on display at retail outlets.

MOBILE PHONES

Phone numbers with the prefixes 04XX are mobiles. Australia's digital network is compatible with GSM 900 and 1800 (used in Europe), but generally not compatible with US or Japanese systems. Mobiles brought from other states of Australia can be used in Sydney, but check your carrier's roaming charges.

COUNTRY & CITY CODES

Australia	☎ 61
Sydney	☎ 02

USEFUL PHONE NUMBERS

International Direct Dial Code	☎ 0011 + country code
International Directory Inquiries	☎ 1225
Interpreters	☎ 13 14 50
Local Directory Inquiries	☎ 12455
Local or International Operator	☎ 1234
Reverse-Charge (collect)	☎ 12550
Time	☎ 1194
Weather	☎ 1196

Television

Sydney has five free-to-air television channels: Channel 2 (which is the government-funded ABC), Channels 7, 9 and 10 (standard commercial fare) and UHF28 (multicultural broadcaster SBS). Cable TV is available free-to-air in most hotels.

Time

Sydney is on Australian Eastern Standard Time, 10 hours ahead of GMT/UTC. Daylight-savings time is one hour ahead of AEST from late-October to March.

Tipping

Most services don't expect tips, but if you're feeling generous tip porters ($2 to $5), waiters (10%) and taxis (10%).

Tourist Information

The **Australian Tourist Commission** (ATC; www.australia.com) conducts customer relations through its efficient website. Sydney has **City Host Information Kiosks** at Circular Quay (5, D4), Town Hall (5, D7) and Martin Place (5, D5). Also try:

Tourism NSW (☎ 13 20 77; www.tourism.nsw.gov.au) State-wide accommodation and travel advice. Airport branch (☎ 9667 6050; ☺ 6am-11.30pm).

Sydney Visitor Centre (5, D3; ☎ 9240 8788; www.sydneyvisitorcentre.com; 106 George St, The Rocks; ☺ 9am-6pm) Super comprehensive, also acting as an accommodation agency. Darling Harbour branch (5, B7; ☎ 9240 8788; ☺ 10am-6pm). Airport branch (☎ 9667 6050).

Travellers' Information Service (5, D9; ☎ 9281 9366; Sydney Coach Terminal, Eddy Ave; ☺ 6am-10.30pm) Helpful, busy office assisting with accommodation bookings, luggage lockers, coach tickets, public transport information and maps.

Tourist Information Service (☎ 9669 5111; ☺ 8am-6pm) Fields phone inquiries.

Women Travellers

Sydney is an egalitarian society and is generally safe for women travellers, although you should avoid walking alone late at night. Sexual harassment and discrimination, while uncommon in Sydney, can occur (usually in the form of infantile sexism from drunks in pubs or bars). The contraceptive pill is available with a doctor's prescription only. Tampons are widely available from supermarkets and chemists.

LANGUAGE

English is the official and dominant language in Australia, but about 20% of people in Sydney speak a different language at home. Australian vernacular ('Strine') can be colourful, hysterical, disarming and bamboozling all at once (see Lonely Planet's *Australian Phrasebook*). Here's a list of essential Strine classics:

arvo – afternoon
barbie – barbecue
beaut, bewdy, bonza – great
bloke – man
bludger – lazy oaf
bugger off – depart with haste (earnest instruction)
crack the shits – to express utmost irritation
crook – ill or substandard
dead horse – tomato sauce, ketchup
dead set – yes, that's correct
dunny – toilet
fair dinkum – honest, genuine
flaming galah – foolish individual
flat out – really busy or fast
footy – football (Australian Rules or Rugby League)
g'day – hello
hard yakka – hard work
having a lend, taking the piss – humorous deception
mate – generic informal address
mozzie – mosquito
no worries, no wukkin furries – everything's under control
ocker, yobbo, bogan – loutish Aussie
ooroo, see ya – goodbye
piss – beer
sheila – woman
shoot through – leave
strewth – annoyed exclamation
tinnie – aluminium boat or beer can
true blue, dinky-di – authentically Australian
tucker – food
youse – more than one person

Index

See also separate indexes for Eating (p125), Sleeping (p126), Shopping (p126) and Sights (p127, includes map references).

EATING

SLEEPING

SHOPPING

Sights Index

FEATURES

Harry's Café de Wheels	*Eating*
State Theatre	*Entertainment*
Tank Stream Bar	*Drinking*
Art Gallery of NSW	*Highlights*
Bondi Beach Market	*Shopping*
Sydney Observatory	*Sights/Activities*
Hotel Altamont	*Sleeping*

AREAS

Beach
Building
Land
Mall
Other Area
Park/Cemetery
Sports

HYDROGRAPHY

River, Creek
Water

BOUNDARIES

State, Provincial
International

ROUTES

Tollway
Freeway
Primary Road
Secondary Road
Tertiary Road
Lane
Under Construction
One-Way Street
Mall/Steps
Tunnel
Walking Path
Walking Trail
Track
Walking Tour

TRANSPORT

Airport, Airfield
Bus Station
Ferry
Monorail
Rail
Taxi Rank
Light Rail

SYMBOLS

Bank, ATM
Beach
Fortress
Christian
Consulate
Hospital, Clinic
Information
Internet Access
Jewish
Lighthouse
Lookout
Monument
Mountain
National Park
Parking Area
Picnic Area
Point of Interest
Police Station
Post Office
Swimming Pool
Telephone
Toilets
Zoo, Wildlife Sanctuary
Waterfall

24/7 travel advice
www.lonelyplanet.com